PAUL ROBESON

By the same author

By Swords Divided: Corfe Castle in the Civil War. Halsgrove, 2003.
Thomas Hardy: Christmas Carollings. Halsgrove, 2005.
Enid Blyton and her Enchantment with Dorset. Halsgrove, 2005.
Tyneham: A Tribute. Halsgrove, 2007.
Agatha Christie: The Finished Portrait. Tempus, 2007.
The Story of George Loveless and the Tolpuddle Martyrs. Halsgrove, 2008.
Father of the Blind: A Portrait of Sir Arthur Pearson. The History Press, 2009.
Agatha Christie: The Pitkin Guide. Pitkin Publishing, 2009.
Arthur Conan Doyle: The Man behind Sherlock Holmes. The History Press, 2009.
HMS Hood: Pride of the Royal Navy. The History Press, 2009.
Purbeck Personalities. Halsgrove, 2009.
Bournemouth's Founders and Famous Visitors. The History Press, 2010.
Thomas Hardy: Behind the Mask. The History Press, 2011.
Hitler: Dictator or Puppet. Pen & Sword Books, 2011.
A Brummie Boy goes to War. Halsgrove, 2011.
Winston Churchill: Portrait of an Unquiet Mind. Pen & Sword Books, 2012.
Charles Darwin: Destroyer of Myths. Pen & Sword Books, 2013.
Beatrix Potter: Her Inner World. Pen & Sword Books, 2013.
T.E. Lawrence: Tormented Hero. Fonthill, 2014.
Agatha Christie: The Disappearing Novelist. Fonthill, 2014.
Lawrence of Arabia's Clouds Hill. Halsgrove, 2014.
Jane Austen: Love is Like a Rose. Fonthill, 2015.
Kindly Light: The Story of Blind Veterans UK. Fonthill, 2015.
Thomas Hardy at Max Gate: The Latter Years. Halsgrove, 2016.
Corfe Remembered. Halsgrove, 2017.
Thomas Hardy: Bockhampton and Beyond. Halsgrove, 2017.
Mugabe: Monarch of Blood and Tears. Austin Macauley, 2017
Making Sense of Marilyn. Fonthill, 2018.
Hitler's Insanity: A Conspiracy of Silence. Fonthill, 2018.
The Unwitting Fundamentalist. Austin Macauley, 2018.
Robert Mugabe's Lost Jewel of Africa. Fonthill, 2018.
Bound for the East Indies: Halsewell – A Shipwreck that Gripped the Nation, Fonthill, 2020.
Beatrix Potter: Her Inner World, Pen & Sword Books, 2020.
The Real Peter Sellers. White Owl 2021

PAUL ROBESON

A SONG FOR FREEDOM

Andrew Norman

NEW HAVEN PUBLISHING LTD

Published 2022
First Edition
NEW HAVEN PUBLISHING LTD
www.newhavenpublishingltd.com
newhavenpublishing@gmail.com

All Rights Reserved
The rights of Andrew Norman, as the author of this work, have been asserted in accordance with the Copyrights, Designs and Patents Act 1988.
No part of this book may be re-printed or reproduced or utilized in any form or by any electronic, mechanical or other means, now unknown or hereafter invented, including photocopying, and recording, or in any information storage or retrieval system, without the written permission of the
Author and Publisher.

Cover image © Library of Congress
Cover Design © George Kalchev

Copyright © 2022 Andrew Norman
All rights reserved
ISBN: 978-1-912587-65-0

Contents

Acknowledgments	8
Author's Note: Some Definitions and Preferences	9
Preface: The Author's First Introduction to Paul Robeson	10
1 Paul Robeson (born 9 April 1898): A Background of Slavery	13
2 Paul's Father, William Drew Robeson	15
3 Paul's Mother, Maria Louisa and her Origins	16
4 The Reverend William Drew Robeson is Ousted from his Post	19
5 The Tragic Death of Paul's mother, Maria Louisa	21
6 Paul's Relationship with his Father	23
7 Princeton, New Jersey (April 1898-1907)	24
8 Westfield, New Jersey (1907-1910): Somerville, New Jersey (1910-1915)	27
9 Paul's Siblings	30
10 Rutgers College, New Brunswick, New Jersey (1915-1917)	34
11 Harlem: Columbia University, New York City (1919-1923): Marriage to Eslanda (1921)	42
12 Eslanda's Background	46
13 The Theatre and Concerts: Paul junior is Born (2 November 1927)	48
14 How Eslanda Helped Her Husband, Paul	53
15 Paul's Alleged Faults	57
16 London (1928-1939)	61
17 Eslanda's Visit to Africa (1936)	69
18 Paul's Attitude to Colonialism	72
19 Return to the USA (1939)	74

20 The Paris Peace Conference (20-24 April 1949): Jackie Robinson	79
21 Further Strivings (1949-1953)	82
22 Eslanda Testifies to the HUAC (7 July 1953)	86
23 Paul Testifies to the HUAC (12 June 1956)	89
24 1956-1958	98
25 Wales: A Welcome in the Valleys for Paul (1957 and 1958)	100
26 Paul Returns to Czechoslovakia (1959)	103
27 1961-1976	107
28 Was Paul Racist?	110
29 Paul's Forebears: Testimony of the Family	112
30 Paul's Grandfather Benjamin who was Held in Slavery	114
31 Paul's Grandmother Sabra who was Held in Slavery	115
32 Temperance Congleton: A Link with the Robersons	116
33 The Geographical Proximity of the Roberson and the Congleton Families	117
34 From what Region of Africa did Benjamin and Sabra's Forebears Originate?	118
35 How and Where did Benjamin and Sabra First Meet?	119
36 Oak Grove Church, Perkins, Pitt County, North Carolina: Another Congleton/Roberson Connection	120
37 Benjamin as a Slave for Hire	121
38 The Birth of William Drew, Ezekiel, and Margaret	122
39 The Identity of the Slave Owner of Sabra and her family	124
40 More About George Outlaw Roberson	126
41 The Escape of William Drew, Ezekiel, and Margaret	128
42 How did William Drew, Ezekiel, and Margaret Effect their Escape? The 'Underground Railroad'	131
43 The American Civil War (12 April 1861 to 9 May 1865): The Contribution made by Blacks	133

44 What Became of Ezekiel and Margaret?	135
45 What Became of Paul's Father, William Drew Robeson	137
46 Were Slave Owners Universally Cruel?	139
47 How Paul's Songs Resonated Throughout the World	141
48 Paul's Final Years: Charlotte Turner Bell	142
49 Paul's Religious Beliefs	147
50 Epilogue	148

Appendix 1
Some of Paul's Lifetime Awards and Recognitions   151

Appendix 2
The Manilla   151

Appendix 3
George Washington's Personal Standard   151

Appendix 4
Evolution of the 'Stars and Stripes'   152

Appendix 5
The Paul Robeson House & Museum, 4951 Walnut Street, Philadelphia, PA.   153

Appendix 6
A Church in Dorset and its Connection with the 'Stars and Stripes'.   153

Appendix 7

Tammy Roberson James, Robersonville, North
Carolina, USA, 6 January 2021   156

Appendix 8

Stephen A. Bess, Rockville, Maryland, USA,
9 January 2021   157

Acknowledgments

A great joy, in my research for this volume, was to make the acquaintance of the following, to whom I am deeply grateful: Tammy Roberson James (great-granddaughter x2 of George O. Roberson); Stephen A. Bess, Associate Professor of English, Montgomery College, Rockville, Maryland (great-grandson of Ezekiel Congleton/Robeson); Vernoca Michael, Executive Director of the West Philadelphia Cultural Alliance and former friend of Paul Robeson.

I am also grateful to Kim Averette; Erin Bradford; Frederick H. Cron; Roger E. Kammerer; William B. Kittrell; Denyse Leslie; Joyce Mosley, a descendant of Cyrus Bustill and Elizabeth Morrey Bustill (Joyce is the author of *Gram's Gift,* a children's book about the contributions made to the history of America by a free African-American family living in Philadelphia during slavery); John A. Oliveti; Barbara Williams; Steve Williams; Leesa Wisdom.

To Jean Bennett and Bernard Burgess, I am grateful for assistance with research, and for discovering much interesting information which would not otherwise have come to light.

Princeton Public Library, Princeton, New Jersey, USA; State Library of North Carolina; Sheppard Memorial Library, Greenville, NC; North Carolina Department of Natural and Cultural Resources, Raleigh, North Carolina; West Philadelphia Cultural Alliance;

Census information and dates for births, marriages and deaths are mainly derived from *Ancestry*.

Author's Note: Some Definitions and Preferences

'Black': belonging to or denoting any human group having dark-coloured skin, especially of African or Australian Aboriginal ancestry.[1] In the context of this narrative, the term 'Black' is taken to refer to Americans and others who have African ancestry.

'Negro': a member of a dark-skinned group of people originally native to Africa south of the Sahara.[2] Although Paul Robeson and his wife, Eslanda ('Essie') both used the term with pride, today it is often regarded as offensive.

'Coloured': a person who is wholly or partly, of non-white descent. In South Africa, a person of mixed descent, usually speaking Afrikaans or English as their mother tongue.[3] Likewise, this term is often regarded as offensive.

The 'Robason' family, which originated in England, plays an integral part in this narrative. However, during the American Civil War, the family changed its surname to 'Roberson', and to avoid confusion, this is the name that will be used hereafter.

After Emancipation, Paul Robeson's father, William Robeson adopted the middle name of 'Drew', and this name will be used hereafter.

1. Stevenson, A., and Waite, M., *Concise Oxford English Dictionary*.
2. Ibid.
3. Ibid.

Preface: The Author's First Introduction to Paul Robeson

When I was a child it was the custom, at weekends, for my family: my father, Chris, my mother, Jean, sister, Jane, and me to have Sunday lunch with 'Nan' (Jane Benwell, my maternal great-grandmother) and her son-in-law, Thomas Waldin ('Tom'), a widower who had been blinded at Ypres during the First World War.

After lunch we were allowed into the front room: hallowed territory; only to be ventured into on a Sunday, and then, only with Nan's express permission. Here, beautiful paintings adorned the walls and there were exquisite china ornaments, including 'piano creepers', little figurines in blue and white which sat atop her pianoforte. Nan also possessed a harmonium.

However, for me, of all the items in the front room, what held the greatest fascination was the cabinet gramophone in the cupboard of which, beneath the turntable, were stored several large cardboard boxes full of 78 rpm records.

Grandad Tom, who had been blinded at Ypres during the First World War, favoured the old army marching songs, such as 'It's a Long Way to Tipperary', and 'The Boys of the Old Brigade'. Both Nan and my mother loved the music of Handel, especially his *Messiah*. As for my father, Chris he was usually too engrossed in his newspaper to notice what was going on.

When my turn came, I made my choice, removed the record carefully from its sleeve, placed it on the turntable, not forgetting (of course) to wind up the gramophone first. Then with infinite care, gently but firmly, I lifted the arm of the gramophone, and delicately placed the needle onto the shining record.

The playing of gramophone records in Nan's front room was often accompanied by a certain amount of background chatter amongst members of the audience. But when that wonderful, unmistakable bass baritone voice of Paul Robeson filled the room, complete silence fell, and even my father lowered his newspaper for the duration of play.

> 'Waterboy, where are you hiding
> If you don't come right here
> Gonna tell you Pa on you …'

And on the reverse side, another favourite, 'Ol' Man River'!

In my younger days, I desperately wanted to sing like Paul, and it grieved me, and still does, that I could not reach the lower notes! Even now, whenever I hear his voice, I feel tears welling up in my eyes. The music and the lyrics stayed with me always; Paul's deep and expressive voice evoking images of the cotton fields of the Deep South (a cultural and geographic sub-region in the southern United States); of the great Mississippi river; of black slaves 'cotton picking' under the hot sun; of toil, of cruelty, of injustice.

But the songs also proved that out of darkness could come immense beauty; of songs sung down through the generations by the slaves and kept alive by Robeson and others to this day, albeit vicariously through his recordings and films.

The 'Negro spiritual' is a religious song of a kind associated with black Christians of the southern USA and thought to derive from the combination of European hymns and African musical elements by black slaves.[1] For the slaves, these 'Spirituals' offered hope: the hope of resurrection, of a better life to come, not in this world, but in the next.

One day, long after the death of our parents, my sister, Jane surprised me by saying that our late father had once heard Paul sing, in the very flesh! We concluded that this must have been on one of the great man's many visits to the UK from the USA.

Also, my wife, Rachel informed me that her late father, Arthur Ernest Jordan, as Dorset Area Organizer for the National Union of Agricultural Workers, had been present in person in August 1958, when Paul visited Wales and sang at the National Eisteddfod (festival of Welsh poetry and music), held in the town of Ebbw Vale. In fact, Arthur had actually shaken hands with Paul!

To the author, as a child, Paul Robeson was a black man from America who sang Negro Spirituals in the most beautiful and expressive male voice that I ever heard (or would ever hear). His songs became part of my DNA!

> 'Joshua fought the battle of Jericho, Jericho, Jericho,
> Joshua fought the battle of Jericho,
> And the walls came a-tumbling down'

Many decades later, I took the opportunity to study the eventful and fascinating life of this son of a slave in detail, and I found the experience to be both rewarding and deeply moving.

1. Stevenson, A., and Waite, M., *Concise Oxford English Dictionary.*

CHAPTER 1

Paul Robeson (born 9 April 1898): A Background of Slavery

Paul Robeson was born on 9 April 1898 in the parsonage of Witherspoon Street Presbyterian Church, Princeton, New Jersey. This was 33 years after slavery was abolished in the USA (in 1865). Paul's parents were the Reverend William Drew Robeson and his wife, Maria Louisa Bustill. There were former slaves on both the maternal and paternal sides of his family.

Yet, Paul emerged from the shadow of slavery to become, arguably, the most energetic and multi-talented advocate for civil rights, racial equality, and social justice in history. And it was not merely the fate of his own African American people which concerned him. He strove on behalf of those from the coal mines and cotton factory 'sweat shops' of the United Kingdom, to the farms and gold mines of South Africa.

Such was the power and majesty of Paul's voice that people could remember exactly where they were and what they were doing when they first heard it: whether live, at one of his concerts in the USA, or on the gramophone or radio thousands of miles away.

In his songs, Paul reminded people of the struggle and suffering of the black American slaves prior to their emancipation. His rendering of the 'Spirituals' offered hope to those who had none. 'Yes we, like Joshua, can bring down the walls of Jericho!'

For Paul, however, this was not enough. He met with trade unionists and addressed them (as a student at Rutgers College, New Jersey, he had won prizes for debate and oratory) and marched with them.

Paul too had his struggles. At Rutgers he was the college's first African-American football player. However, on the football field, as a black man he was subjected to brutality. Nevertheless, as a star athlete he persevered, and from 1920 to 1922 played in the newly-founded National Football League (NFL). Similarly, when the Ku Klux Clan disrupted his concerts, he simply rescheduled them.

Paul believed that Soviet Russia offered it's citizens a better, fairer deal, and he made no secret of this. As a result, the 'McCarthy Era' of political witch hunts against alleged Communists in the USA, he was summoned to appear before the House's Un-American Activities Committee. The HUAC, however, quickly discovered that it was *he* who was interrogating *them* and challenging *their* beliefs. Paul completely turned the tables, used the event as a platform to put forward his views on social justice, and on so doing, tied his would-be interrogators up in proverbial knots! And as the son of a slave, his credentials for so doing were impeccable.

Paul possessed many gifts. At college, he had been accepted into the Phi Beta Kappa: the oldest academic honorary society in the USA; and into the Cap and Skull, a senior honorary society at Rutgers for excellence in academic achievement, athletics, the arts, and public service.

He was a qualified lawyer, having graduated from Columbia University. He had studied and was familiar with 40 or so languages; he could play the piano. Above all, he knew how to inspire people; the miners of South Wales, for example, when he visited them in the late 1950s.

Paul was both actor and film star. For example, he played the part of 'Othello' in the eponymous play by William Shakespeare, both in London's West End with the Royal Shakespeare Company at Stratford-on-Avon and on Broadway, in a record run of 296 performances! He starred as 'Joe' in the musical *Show Boat*, and as 'David Goliath' in the film, *Proud Valley*.

Most importantly, Paul met and married the hugely talented Eslanda, herself the descendant of slaves. She shared his views and supported him through the good and bad times.

As an author, the challenge for me was to see if I could make contact with any of Paul's descendants, and any descendants of his slave owner, who might have unique information about the Robeson family, and to find out where exactly his father William and mother Maria had been enslaved. The search was a fruitful one, beyond my wildest dreams, as the reader will discover!

CHAPTER 2

Paul's Father, William Drew Robeson

Paul described William Drew thus: 'Though my father was a man of ordinary height, he was very broad of shoulder and his physical bearing reflected the rock-like strength and dignity of his character. He had the greatest speaking voice I have ever heard. It was a deep, sonorous basso, richly melodic and refined, vibrant with the love and compassion which filled him'.[1]

William Drew and Maria Louisa had five surviving children, all of whom were born in Princeton. They were: William Drew Robeson junior (born 1881); (John Bunyan) Reeve Robeson (born 1885); Benjamin Congleton Robeson (born 1893); Marian Margaret Robeson (born 1894).

The last child, the subject of this narrative, was a son, born on 9 April 1898, 'when the Reverend Robeson was a vigorous man of fifty-three and his wife a partially blind invalid of forty-five'.[2] They named him Paul Leroy Robeson.

---

1. Robeson, Paul, with Lloyd L. Brown, *Here I Stand*, pp.8-9.
2. Robeson, Eslanda Goode, *Paul Robeson: Negro*, p.23

CHAPTER 3

Paul's Mother, Maria Louisa and her Origins

Maria Louisa (née Bustill), wife of the Reverend William Drew Robeson and mother of Paul Robeson, was born on 8 November 1853 at Philadelphia, Pennsylvania.

In *Paul Robeson Negro*, Paul's wife, Eslanda described Maria Louisa (the name by which the family knew her) as 'a tall, slender woman of distinctly Indian type, with very straight black hair, brown skin, and clear brown eyes; she was highly intellectual, with an alert mind and a very remarkable memory; she was rather quiet, and deeply religious'.[2] In fact, Maria Louisa's paternal great-grandmother x2 was of Delaware Indian heritage.

Said Paul and Eslanda's son and only child, Paul junior, 'Maria Louisa was tall and handsome. She was known for her gentle, compassionate, sunny disposition'. She served 'as William Drew's intellectual companion, helped him compose his sermons, and acted as his right hand in his community work'.[3]

Eslanda waxed lyrical about Maria Louisa's, family, and not without good reason, for they included people of no mean achievement and distinction. And this was all the more remarkable because slaves were numbered among their ancestors.

Said Eslanda, 'The Bustill family is one of the most widely known and highly respected Negro families in early Philadelphia; they trace their ancestry back as far as 1608, along Indian-Quaker-Negro stock, and all along the line find distinguished men and women of whom they are justly proud'.

For example, Humphrey Morrey (1640-1716) was asked by William Penn (English Quaker reformer, colonialist, and founder of Pennsylvania) to be the first mayor of Philadelphia, in which capacity he served from 1691 to 1701.

Cyrus Bustill (1732-1806) was the son of Samuel Bustill (a prominent Quaker lawyer living in Burlington, NJ) and Parthenia, who was one of his father's slaves and of African descent. Cyrus was duly freed from slavery ('manumitted') in 1769. Whereupon, he moved to Philadelphia and built up a business as a baker.[4] During the Revolutionary War (1775-1783), Cyrus 'baked bread for George Washington's [Continental] troops'.[5]

In *Paul Robeson: Negro*, Eslanda stated that Cyrus Bustill 'was one of the most active workers for the religious, moral, and intellectual progress of his people; he was one of the founders of the Free African Society, which was the first beneficial society organized by Negroes in America'.

Free African Society, founded 10 April 1787: a benevolent organization that held religious services and provided mutual aid for 'free Africans and their descendants' in Philadelphia.

By the year 1791, Cyrus 'was recorded as owning twelve acres of land in the black settlement of Guineatown, between the Abingdon and Cheltenham townships of Montgomery County, Pennsylvania'.[6] Beginning in 1802, the talented and enterprising Cyrus operated a school out of his house.[7]

David Bustill Bowser (1820-1900) was a portrait painter of note, who painted twenty-one portraits of Abraham Lincoln; for one of which Lincoln posed in person.[8]

David was given the honour of painting flags for each of the 11 black Union regiments that fought in the Civil War. He himself was a member of one such regiment.

Only one of these flags survives: that of the 127th US Colored Infantry Regiment and it has been purchased by the Atlanta History Center, Atlanta, Georgia. 'The flag depicts a black soldier waving goodbye to Columbia, a white woman representing America. In the painting, Columbia is holding an American flagpole. Ribboned across the top is the motto: "We Will Prove Ourselves Men".'[9]

Joseph Casey Bustill (1822-1895). A highly educated person, Joseph became 'one of the youngest members of the famous 'Underground Railroad Chain' and aided over a thousand fugitive slaves to freedom'.[10] That, at least, would have pleased Eslanda's husband, Paul!

When Eslanda's biography, *Paul Robeson; Negro* was published in 1930, Paul was not entirely pleased. In *The Undiscovered Paul Robeson*, Paul junior, wrote of the biography as follows: 'At the outset of her book she paid extended homage to Paul's elite Bustill ancestry, from which he himself felt alienated, while only briefly mentioning his slave Robeson ancestors, with whom he closely identified. Paul was particularly annoyed by her substitution of the name "Bustill" for his actual middle name "Leroy".'[11]

One wonders if, by dwelling on the achievements of the Bustills, Eslanda was being a little mischievous, teasing Paul, and at the same time attempting to goad him into greater activity!

1. Robeson, Eslanda Goode, *Paul Robeson: Negro,* p.23.
2. Ibid, p.23.
3. Robeson, Paul, Jr., *The Undiscovered Paul Robeson: An Artist's Journey,* 1898-1939, p.4.
4. *Wikipedia.*
5. Princeton Public Library, Robeson ancestry online.
6. *Wikipedia.*
7. Information kindly supplied by Joyce Mosley.
8. Robeson, Eslanda Goode, *Paul Robeson: Negro,* op. cit., p.22.
9. Bellows, Kate, 'Atlanta History Center purchases black Union regiment's flag for $196,800', Pennsylvania Real-Time News, PA PENNLIVE Patriot-News, 14 June 2019.
100. Robeson, Eslanda Goode, *Paul Robeson: Negro,* op. cit., p.22.
11. Robeson, Paul, Jr., *The Undiscovered Paul Robeson: An Artist's Journey,* 1898-1939, op. cit., p.171.

CHAPTER 4

The Reverend William Drew Robeson is Ousted from his Post

Sadly, for William Drew, said Paul, a 'grievous blow' was to befall him when, after two decades of service to his church, 'a factional dispute among the members removed him as pastor' of Witherspoon Street Presbyterian Church.[1] And so, on 27 January 1901, William Drew preached his last sermon to that congregation. The Robeson family were, therefore, obliged 'to leave the comfortable Witherspoon Street parsonage and move to a smaller house on Green Street, around the corner'.[2]

Almost six decades later, Paul stated that the Witherspoon Street Presbyterian Church 'still stands, with one of the stained glass windows glowing "In Loving Remembrance of Sabra Robeson" who was my father's slave mother on the Carolina plantation'.[3]

Plantation: a large estate on which crops such as coffee, sugar, and tobacco are grown.[4]

The installation of this beautiful window by the Reverend William Drew Robeson was a measure of his deep and abiding love for his mother, Sabra.

'Adding to the pain', said Paul, 'was the fact that some of his father's 'closest kin were part of the ousting faction. A gentle scholar and teacher all his adult life, my father, then past middle age, with an invalid wife and dependent children at home, was forced to begin life anew. He got a horse and a wagon and began to earn his living hauling ashes for the townsfolk'.[5]

'A fond memory remains of our horse, a mare named Bess, whom I grew to love and who loved me. My father also went into the hack business, and as a coachman drove the gay young students around town and on trips to the seashore. Ash-man, coachman, he was still the dignified Reverend Robeson to the community, and no man carried himself with greater pride. Not once did I hear him complain of the poverty and misfortune of those years. Not one word of bitterness ever came from him. Serene, undaunted, he struggled to earn a livelihood and see to our education.'[6]

1. Robeson, Paul, with Lloyd L. Brown, *Here I Stand*, pp.8-11.
2. Robeson, Paul, Jr. *The Undiscovered Paul Robeson: An Artist's Journey, 1898-1939*, p.6.
3. Robeson, Paul, with Lloyd L. Brown, *Here I Stand*, p.7.
4. Stevenson, A., and Waite, M., *Concise Oxford English Dictionary*.
5. Robeson, Paul, with Lloyd L. Brown, *Here I Stand*, op. cit., p.12.
6. Ibid, p.12.

CHAPTER 5

The Tragic Death of Paul's mother, Maria Louisa

When Paul was aged 5, tragedy struck. Said Eslanda, 'On the fatal morning of 19 January 1904, the Reverend Robeson went to Trenton on business'. As for the children, '"W. D." [William Drew Robeson junior] and Reeve were at college, Marian and Paul were at school, and Benjamin remained at home with his mother to help her clean the living-room of the parsonage'.

'Mrs Robeson had been suffering for years with asthma and with eye trouble. She wore thick glasses, but these had not been much help because cataracts were rapidly growing and almost completely destroying her sight. On this particular morning she felt well, however, and decided, with her customary housewifely thoroughness, to make a good job of cleaning the room. She decided first, to take up the carpet, but the stove was in the way. She and Ben conferred about it and decided she would lift the stove by the legs, while he pulled away the carpet from underneath. The stove had a sliding front door, which opened as she raised the front legs, and a hot coal fell out.'

The outcome was that Marie Louisa's dress caught fire, and 'her feet, legs and hands were horribly burned; part of her hair was burned off, and she had even swallowed some of the flame'.

'The neighbours and parishioners who loved and admired her, gathered at her bedside helplessly, and there found more reason to love and admire her. She told them not to pity her: "This is the way I am to go", she said courageously, and because God intended it, I am content".'

When her husband, William Drew arrived, 'shocked and heart-broken, she told him with her beautiful faith not to wish it had been otherwise, that it was God's will; she thanked him for his love and asked him to see that their children did not forget her teachings. Then, overcome with pain, she concentrated her thoughts on God, and recited the First and Twenty-Third Psalms over and over to soothe herself. The doctors gave her opiates, and she lapsed into unconsciousness and died'.[1] The date of Louise's death was 20 January 1904.

Said Paul of his mother, 'I was 6 [actually 5] years old when she, a near-blind invalid at the time, was fatally burned in a household accident. I remember her lying in the coffin, and the funeral, and the relatives who came, but it must be that the pain and shock of her death blotted out all other personal recollections. Others have told me of her remarkable intellect; her strength of character and spirit, which contributed so much to my father's development and work. She was a companion to him in his studies; she helped compose his sermons; she was his right hand in all his community work'.[2]

Said Eslanda, 'Soon after his wife's death, the Reverend Robeson moved to Westfield, New Jersey, taking his youngest child, Paul with him'.[3]

1. Robeson, Eslanda Goode, *Paul Robeson: Negro,* pp.24-5.
2. Robeson, Paul, with Lloyd L. Brown, *Here I Stand,* p.7.
3. Robeson, Eslanda Goode, *Paul Robeson: Negro,* op. cit., p.25.

CHAPTER 6

Paul's Relationship with his Father

The 'text' of his father, William Drew Robeson's life, said Paul, was 'loyalty to one's convictions. Unbending. Despite anything. From youngest days I was imbued with that concept. This bedrock idea of integrity was taught by Reverend Robeson to his children, not so much by preachment (for by nature Pop was restrained of speech, often silent at home, and among us Robesons the deepest feelings are largely unexpressed in words) but rather, by the daily example of his life and work'.

'How proudly, as a boy, I walked at his side, my hand in his, as he moved among the people! There was a wide gap in years between us — he was 53 when I was born; near 60 when my mother died — but during many of his years as a widower I was the only child at home, and his devoted care and attention bound us closely together. It was not like him to be demonstrative in his love, nor was he quick to praise. Doing the right thing – well, that was something to be taken for granted in his children. I knew what I must do - when to come home from play, my duties in the household, my time for study – and I readily yielded to his quiet discipline.'[1]

Only once did Paul disobey his father, and he felt guilty about it ever after!

---

1. Robeson, Paul, with Lloyd L. Brown, *Here I Stand*, pp.8-9.

CHAPTER 7

Princeton, New Jersey (April 1898-1907)

What did Paul think about living in Princeton, NJ, where he spent the first 9 years of his life? Said he bitterly, 'Rich Princeton was white: the Negroes were there to do the work. An aristocracy must have its retainers, and so the people of our small Negro community were, for the most part, a servant class: domestics in the homes of the wealthy, serving as cooks and waiters; caretakers at the university; coachmen for the town, and laborers at the nearby farms and brickyards. I had the closest of ties with these workers, since many of my father's relatives - Uncle Ben and Uncle John, and Cousin Carraway and Cousin Chance and others - had come to this town and found employment at such jobs'.

'Princeton was Jim Crow', said Paul.

'Jim Crow': the former practice of segregating black people in the US.[1]

Years later, Paul described Princeton as 'a college town of southern aristocrats, who from Revolutionary time [the time of the Revolutionary War, 1775-1783], transferred [from] Georgia to New Jersey'.

Georgia: state in the south-eastern region of the US.

'Almost every Negro in Princeton lived off the college and accepted the social status that went with it. We lived, for all intents and purposes, on a southern plantation. And with no more dignity than that suggests - all the bowing and scraping to the drunken rich; all the vile names; all the Uncle Tomming to earn enough to lead miserable lives.'[2]

'The grade [elementary] school that I attended was segregated and Negroes were not permitted in any high school. My eldest brother, Bill had to travel to Trenton - 11 miles away - to attend high school, and I would have had to do the same had we not moved to another town. No Negro students were admitted to the university, although one or two were allowed to attend the divinity school.'

'Under the caste system in Princeton the Negro, restricted to menial jobs at low pay and lacking any semblance of political rights or bargaining power, could hope not for justice, but for charity. The stern hearts and tight purses of the master class could, on occasion, be opened by appeals from the "deserving poor", and then philanthropy in the form of donations, small loans, or cast-off clothing, might be looked for.'

'The Negro church, center of community life, was the main avenue through which such boons were sought and received, and, in fact, the Witherspoon Street Presbyterian Church was itself largely built by white philanthropy. The pastor was a sort-of bridge between the Have-nots and the Haves, and he served his flock in many worldly ways - seeing work for the jobless, money for the needy, mercy from the Law.'

Paul saved his most withering criticism for Woodrow Wilson, President of Princeton University, who had declared that it was 'impossible' for Paul's brother, Ben to attend that institution. Woodrow Wilson, 28th (Democratic) President of the USA from 1913 to 1921 was, said Paul sarcastically, a 'Nobel Peace Prize winner, apostle of the New Liberalism, advocate of democracy for the world and Jim Crow for America!'

What was Paul's father, William Drew's reaction to having to live in such an environment? Said Paul, 'He who comes hat-in-hand is expected to bow and bend, and so I marvel that there was no hint of servility in my father's make-up. Just as in youth he had refused to remain a slave, so in all the years of his manhood he disdained to be an Uncle Tom. From him we learned, and never doubted it, that the Negro was in every way the equal of the white man. And we fiercely resolved to prove it'.

For Paul, however, life at Princeton was not all doom, gloom, and racial discrimination. Said he, 'Because I was younger, my own days in Princeton were happier ones. Mostly I played. There were the vacant lots for ball games, and the wonderful moments when Bill, vacationing from college where he played on the team, would teach me how to play football. He was my first coach, and over and over again on a weed-grown lot he would put me through the paces: how to tackle a man so he stayed tackled; how to run with the ball. Then there were the winter evenings at home with Pop: he loved to play checkers and so we two would sit for hours in the parlor, engrossed in our game, not speaking much but wonderfully happy together'.

'Not old enough to work for them', said Paul sarcastically, 'I had very little connection with the white people of Princeton; but there were some white children among my playmates. One of these was a boy, about my age, whose father owned the neighbourhood grocery, a few doors from our house. We could not go to school together, of course, but during the long summer days we were inseparable companions at play. Once - and I don't remember why - the two of us got into a small-boy fight. After much crouching and circling and menacing gestures, we each got up enough courage to land a blow on the other's nose and then, wailing loudly, we ran away to our homes. Next day we were friends again.'

'There must have been moments when I felt the sorrows of a motherless child, but what I most remember from my youngest days was an abiding sense of comfort and security. I got plenty of mothering, not only from Pop and my brothers and sister when they were home, but from the whole of our close-knit community. Across the street and down each block were all my aunts and uncles and cousins — including some who were not actual relatives at all. So, if I were to try to put down the names of all the folks who helped raise me, it would read like a roster of Negro Princeton. In a way I was "adopted" by all these good people, and there was always a place at their tables and a place in a bed (often with two or three other young ones) for Reverend Robeson's boy, when my father was away on one of his trips to the seashore, or attending a church conference.'[3]

Paul would return to the theme of the 'Motherless Child', which he himself had been since the age of 5.

In 1907, when Paul was aged 9, the family left Princeton for Westfield, New Jersey.

---

1. Stevenson, A., and Waite, M., *Concise Oxford English Dictionary*.
2. Foner, Philip S., *Paul Robeson Speaks*, p.201
3. Robeson, Paul, with Lloyd L. Brown, *Here I Stand*, pp.10-15.

CHAPTER 8

Westfield, New Jersey (1907-1910): Somerville, New Jersey (1910-1915)

The town of Westfield, New Jersey, is situated some 30 miles to the north-east of Princeton. Said Paul, 'For years in Princeton, after he lost his church, friends had told my father that he must return to preaching. And so, at the age of 62, when he got the chance, he eagerly set out to begin all over again. Now, he joined a different denomination: the African Methodist Episcopal Zion [AME Zion] Church.'

'Westfield, though larger than Princeton, had a much smaller black population, of whom fewer than a dozen were adherents of the AME Zion denomination. Together with that little band of followers', the Reverend Robeson 'dug the foundation for the church building that would rise when and if, the money could be raised. As the Bishop who assigned him to that unpromising post must have known, William Robeson was a remarkable fund-raiser'. Then, 'the seemingly impossible task' was accomplished, 'and in 1908, a year after Rev. Robeson's arrival, the St Luke's AME Zion Church was erected, together with a parsonage for the wonder-working pastor'.[1]

Said Paul, 'there were too few children for the town to have a separate school "for colored only", so the grade school I attended during the three years we lived there was mixed [i.e. unsegregated]'.[2]

The discovery that Paul had 'a talent for singing ... was said to have been made one day at the parsonage when the three brothers were singing popular ballads in harmony. Out of all the discord, Bill yelled: "Wait a minute, hit that note again, Paul". Paul hit it out of the lot (the baseball expression for a home run still came naturally to the former boyhood baseball star), and Bill said: "Paul, you can sing". Paul ridiculed the idea at first, but at Bill's insistence he began to sing with the church choir and at their home performances'.[3]

In 1910 the Robeson family relocated once again, this time to Somerville, New Jersey, situated 'midway between Westfield and Princeton'.[4] Here, 'they found a fine church [of St Thomas] and parsonage awaiting them'.[5]

As had been the case in Westfield, Paul found the atmosphere vis-à-vis 'Negro' and 'White' to be 'not so rigid'. 'I came to know more white people', he said. 'I frequently visited the homes of my schoolmates and always received a friendly welcome.' However, 'I wasn't conscious of it at the time, but now I realize that my easy moving between the two racial communities was rather exceptional.'

'I attended eighth grade' at Somerville High School (which was entirely for Blacks) 'and graduated at the head of my class' said Paul. 'Pop was pleased by that, I guess.' Paul's father, William Drew, however, was determined that his children should make the best of themselves. 'I have often told how he was never satisfied with a school mark of 95 when 100 was possible. But this was not because he made a fetish of perfection. Rather, it was that the concept of *personal integrity*, which was his ruling passion, included inseparably the idea of *maximum human fulfillment*. Success in life was not to be measured in terms of money and personal advancement, but rather the goal must be the richest and highest development of one's own potential. A love for learning, a ceaseless quest for truth in all its fullness – this my father taught.' And his son, Paul did not let him down!

'High school in Somerville was not Jim Crow', said Paul, 'and there I formed close friendships with a number of white classmates. I was welcomed as a member of the Glee Club (unlike later at college) and the drama club and into the various sports and social activities around the school'.

Glee Club: a society for singing part-songs.

Part-song: a secular song with three or more voice parts, typically unaccompanied.[6]

However, although Paul sang at the Glee Club, he was not permitted to accompany the club to out-of-town concerts.[7]

'The teachers also were friendly and several of them are especially remembered. Miss Vosseller, the music teacher who directed our Glee Club, took a special interest in training my voice. Anna Miller, English teacher, paid close attention to my development as a speaker and debater; and it was she who first introduced me to Shakespeare's works. Many years were to pass before the American theatre would permit a Negro to play *Othello*. Miss Vandeveer, who taught Latin, seemed to have no taint of racial prejudice; and Miss Bagg, instructor in chemistry and physics, made every effort to make me feel welcome and at ease in the school's social life of which she was in charge. Miss Bagg urged me to attend the various parties and dances, and when I did so, it was she who was the first to dance with me. But despite her encouragement, I shied away from most of these social affairs.'[8]

For in the mind of Paul lurked feelings of uncertainty, mistrust, and reservation. 'There was always the feeling that - well, something unpleasant might happen; for the two worlds of White and Negro were nowhere more separate than in social life. Though I might visit the homes of white classmates, I was always conscious that I belonged to the Negro community.'[9]

Subsequently, said Eslanda, Paul 'was Superintendent of the Sunday School and often helped his father with the services. He led the singing in church with his big, unmanageable, but beautifully moving bass voice, and was often carried away by the religious emotion which swept the congregation with the music. He became an essential part of the church and, in turn, the church, the music, and the people became an essential part of him. So that later, it was entirely natural that he should be able to sing the lovely music of these lowly people in all its glorious simplicity. Audiences felt, when he sang the songs, that they were really a part of him, as indeed they were'.[10]

1. Brown, Lloyd L., *The Young Paul Robeson: On My Journey Now*, p.35.
2. Robeson, Paul, with Lloyd L. Brown, *Here I Stand*, pp.16-17.
3. Brown, Lloyd L., *The Young Paul Robeson: On My Journey Now*, op. cit., p.38.
4. Robeson, Paul, with Lloyd L. Brown, *Here I Stand*, op. cit., p.18.
5. Robeson, Eslanda Goode, *Paul Robeson: Negro,* p.26.
6. Stevenson, A., and Waite, M., *Concise Oxford English Dictionary.*
7. *'Paul Robeson: Here I Stand', PBS American Masters, 1999.
8. Robeson, Paul, with Lloyd L. Brown, *Here I Stand*, op. cit., p.19.
9. Ibid, pp.19-20.
10. Robeson, Eslanda Goode, *Paul Robeson: Negro,* op. cit., pp.29-30.

CHAPTER 9

Paul's Siblings

Said Paul's friend, Lloyd L. Brown, 'At the time Paul was born [on 9 April 1898] his brother, Ben and his sister, Marian were still too young for school, but his brother, Reeve ... was enrolled in the segregated Witherspoon Street Public School. Paul's older brother, Bill [William Drew junior], was attending high school, but because black students were barred from the secondary school in Princeton, Bill had to travel to Trenton each day [12 miles to the south] to get the education the Rev. Robeson sought for his children'.[1]

At the time of the children's mother, Maria Louisa's death on 20 January 1904, said Lloyd L. Brown, 'The two oldest sons – Bill, who was 22, and Reeve, 18 – were away at college (Bill at the University of Pennsylvania Medical School and Reeve at Lincoln University - of which both his father and Bill were alumni); and the girl [daughter], Marian who was 9, was in class at nearby Witherspoon Street Public School'.[2]

Said Paul, 'Pop sent my brother, Ben away to prep school and Biddle University in North Carolina, and my sister, Marian to [Barber-] Scotia Seminary [Concord, NC], a school for colored girls in the same state'.[3]

William ('Bill') Drew Robeson junior (born 8 November 1881, Princeton, NJ)

Said Paul, it was to Bill 'the oldest, to whom the other children of the Reverend Robeson gave first place as far as brains were concerned.[4] 'During my high school years in Somerville, Bill was often at home, between colleges and railroad runs, and he spent much time directing my studies.'[5]

Said Lloyd L. Brown, 'Circumstances, as well as his own inclination, made Bill the perennial student. A lack of money had caused him to drop out of medical school at Penn [the Perelman School of Medicine – 'Penn Med' – of the University of Pennsylvania, Philadelphia], which he had entered after graduating from Lincoln'. (Paul junior, however, stated that Bill had also dropped out of Lincoln 'at the start of his senior year'.[6]

Brown continued, 'and then, after supporting himself by working as a Pullman porter and a railroad station redcap [porter], he began again at medical college in Boston. However, after graduating from that school, Bill was dismayed to learn that he was not qualified to practise medicine in New Jersey or New York because the Boston school was not accredited elsewhere. For Bill, there was only one thing to do: start all over again at yet another medical school. Finally, in 1921, at the age of 39, and after four years of study at Howard University College of Medicine in Washington DC, William D. Robeson Jr was awarded his long-sought MD'.[7]

Howard University: founded 1867, for Blacks.

On 10 October 1925, Bill married Beatrice Cline.

John Bunyan Reeve Robeson (born 10 March 1886, Princeton, NJ)

Reeve, sadly, did not live up to his father's expectations. Said Lloyd L. Brown, 'The circumstances of Reeve's failure', when he left Lincoln University without a degree, 'are not known'. However, 'If, as may happen with a preacher's son, Reeve had become surfeited with the religious environment at home, he would have found no change at college. Lincoln University, like other church-sponsored colleges for Blacks, made chapel attendance compulsory, and there was little exaggeration in the complaint of the students that chapel was three times every day and all day Sunday'.

The outcome was, said Brown, that Reeve returned home 'without a college diploma' and 'got a horse and carriage and became a hack driver'. However, Reeve 'lacked the iron self-control that such a job required'.

'Scorning the social laws of caste behaviour, the rebellious Reeve became increasingly scornful of law in general, and from time to time it became the embarrassing duty of the dignified Rev. Robeson to go to court and try to get his son out of trouble.'

To 'young Paul' however, 'that wayward brother, so quick with his fists to challenge any slight, was as admirable as Bill, who was always best in his classes; or Ben, star of the neighbourhood with a baseball and bat'.[8] Paul himself, said of Reeve, 'He won no honours in classroom, pulpit, or platform. Yet I remember him with love. Restless, rebellious, scoffing at conventions, defiant of the white man's law. "Don't ever take low", was the lesson Reed taught me. "Stand up to them and hit back harder than they hit you!".'[9] In other words, do not accept that you are in any way inferior to white people.

In 1910 the 24-year-old Reeve was living as a lodger in Detroit, Michigan, and working as a waiter in a hotel.

On 1 June 1941, Reeve married Ruby Jean Nichols at Dakota City, Dakota, Nebraska.

Marian Margaret Robeson (born 1 December 1894, Princeton, NJ)

Of his sister Marian, Paul said, 'As a girl she brought to our household the blessing of laughter, so filled is she with warm good humour'.[10]

Marian attended a training school for teachers in West Chester, Pennsylvania.[11] In 1931 she married Dr William Alexander Forsythe of Philadelphia. In 1933 she bore him a daughter, Paulina.

Benjamin Congleton Robeson (born 19 September 1894, Princeton, NJ)

(By giving their child this middle name, his father, William Drew was clearly anxious to preserve 'Congleton' as a family name, indicating, perhaps, that he looked on his former slave owner without malice.)

Said Paul, 'It was my brother, Ben who most inspired my interest in sports. Ben was an outstanding athlete by any standards, and had he attended one of the prominent colleges I'm convinced he would have been chosen All-American'.[12]

All-American: honoured as one of the best amateur competitors in the USA.[13]

During the First World War, Benjamin served with the 369th Infantry Regiment as military chaplain. On 8 June 1918 he married Frances Elizabeth Cline, who bore him three children.

Benjamin became pastor at the Mother AME Zion Church in Harlem, New York City (NYC). Founded in 1796, this is the oldest African American church in the state of New York. It was established when black parishioners left John Street Methodist Church in that city. The group, under the leadership of Minister James Varick, had grown disillusioned with increasing segregationist practices within the Methodist church organization.[14]

1. Brown, Lloyd L., *The Young Paul Robeson: On My Journey Now*, p.21
2. Ibid, p.28.
3. Robeson, Paul, with Lloyd L. Brown, *Here I Stand*, p.12.
4. Ibid, p.21.

5. Ibid, p.22.
6. Robeson, Paul, Jr., *The Undiscovered Paul Robeson: An Artist's Journey,* 1898-1939, p.12.
7. Brown, Lloyd L., *The Young Paul Robeson: On My Journey Now*, op. cit., p.45.
8. Ibid, pp.33-4.
9. Robeson, Paul, with Lloyd L. Brown, *Here I Stand*, op. cit., p.13
10. Ibid, p.23.
11. Brown, Lloyd L., *The Young Paul Robeson: On My Journey Now*, op. cit., p.32.
12. Robeson, Paul, with Lloyd L. Brown, *Here I Stand*, op. cit., p.22.
13. Stevenson, A., and Waite, M., *Concise Oxford English Dictionary.*
14. *Wikipedia.*

CHAPTER 10

Rutgers College, New Brunswick, New Jersey (1915-1917)

When Paul was in his senior year at Somerville High School, he said, he 'learnt about a competitive examination open to all students in New Jersey; the prize - a four-year scholarship to Rutgers College'.

Rutgers: New Brunswick, Middlesex County, New Jersey, named after the American Revolutionary War colonel, Henry Rutgers (1745-1830).

The college, said Paul, 'was only 15 miles away' and it was 'one of the oldest in America', having been founded in 1766. It was also 'considered rather exclusive; and while one or two Negroes had once been admitted, none had attended Rutgers for many years'.[1]

The outcome was, that Paul won the scholarship. 'Here was a decisive point in my life', he declared. 'That I would go to Rutgers was the least of it, for I was sure I'd be happier at Lincoln [the University that both his father and his brother, Bill had attended]. The important thing was this: *Deep in my heart from that day on was a conviction which none of the Ackermans of America would ever be able to shake.* Equality might be denied, but I *knew* I was not inferior.'[2] This was a reference to Dr William A. Ackerman, Principal of Somerville High School, who had been 'consistently so hostile' to Paul.[3]

During the summer of 1915, Paul and his brother, Ben worked as waiters at a hotel in Narragansett, Rhode Island.[4]

It was in the 'fall of 1915', said Paul 'when I entered college to learn more Latin and Greek, more Physics and Math[s], more History which included neither Toussaint nor Phillips - and to play a little football, too'. This was an understatement!

Toussaint Louverture (1743-1803): Haitian general who led a slave revolt against the French in their colony of Saint-Domingue (Haiti).

Wendell Phillips (1811-1884): white US abolitionist and social reformer.

'As I went out into life, one thing loomed above all else: I was my father's son, a Negro in America. That was the challenge'.[5]

Said Eslanda of Paul, 'As soon as he settled down to the routine of college life, he began to try out for the various athletics teams. In many of the big American universities football has assumed an enormous importance; it is a signal honour to be a member of the 'varsity; "the team" is a group apart - almost a sacred group. Football games are now national events and crowds as large as 70, 80, and 90 thousand people view the big matches'.[6]

However, when Paul 'tried out for the team in 1915, he met with many disappointments. He was a tall, awkward boy of 17'. Whereas 'the team was made up mostly, of great six foot two, and six foot three-inch men with an average weight of two hundred and ten pounds'. Not only that, but 'each man realised that he might not only lose his place in the sacred eleven, but he might lose it to a Negro. So, the practice games became hard fought. But Paul was a natural athlete, a fine football player, and his eligibility became more and more obvious'.

'Because he was the most formidable man in the "scrub", the team began to concentrate their plays against him.'

Scrub: a team made up of players who were neither in the varsity squad nor the regular team.

'The playing became bitter; play after play was made against him until he was tired out.' In consequence of this, Paul suffered a broken nose and a dislocated shoulder, and 'was always badly battered when he emerged from each scrimmage'.[7]

Scrimmage: an imaginary transverse line beyond which a team may not venture until the next play has begun.

Nevertheless, remembering the example of his father, William Drew, Paul battled on. Said he, 'I had 10 days in bed; a few days at the training table, and then out for another scrimmage. I made a tackle and was on the ground, my right-hand palm down on the ground. A boy came over and stepped hard on my hand. He meant to break the bones. The bones held, but his cleats took every single one of the fingernails off my right hand. That's when I knew rage!'

Cleat: projection on the sole of a boot.[8]

'The next play came around my end, the whole first-string backfield came at me. I swept out my arms, and the three men running interference went down, they just went down.'

Interference: a foul that occurs on an eligible receiver, impeding him in his fair attempt to catch a forward pass.

'The ball carrier was a first-class back named Kelly. I wanted to kill him, and I meant to kill him. It wasn't a thought, it was just feeling, to kill. I got Kelly in my two hands and I got him up over my head. I was going to smash him so hard to the ground that I'd break him right in two, and I could have done it. But just then the coach yelled, the first thing came to his mind, he yelled, "Robey, you're on the varsity!" That brought me around. We laughed about it often later. They all got to be my friends.'[9]

This says much about the character of Paul, doggedly determined in the face of violent and brutal provocation, and yet willing to forgive.

Eslanda continued, 'Paul was active in other sports at Rutgers; he was catcher in the 'varsity baseball team; centre in the basketball team; he threw the discus for the track team. He was always in training. When the football season ended at Thanksgiving and the rest of the team broke training, Paul join the basketball squad and began at once, to train with them; at the end of the basketball season in the spring, he joined the baseball squad'.

Thanksgiving: an annual holiday marked by religious observances and a traditional meal, held in the USA on the fourth Thursday in November.[10]

'He played all games brilliantly, and the student body found itself always cheering for "Robey" when it was cheering for Rutgers'.[11]

During his time at college, said Eslanda, 'Paul went home to Somerville at least once a week to see his father. They had long talks, as of old, and the father listened attentively to the accounts of his son's life at the university. "You mustn't forget your studies for your game, son; you went to school to study, not to play. I'm glad that you can play, but you mustn't forget the real reason why you went to college." Paul would smile and show his father his grades. His averages were usually about 95% and his father was delighted.' Nevertheless, in respect of sport, the 'old man loved games, and availed himself of every opportunity to see his son play'.

At the end of Paul's junior year, said Eslanda, his average grades 'were so high that he was elected to Phi Beta Kappa, an honour which few students achieve until their senior year, and the vast majority never achieve at all'.

Phi Beta Kappa: an honorary society of undergraduates and some graduates, to which members are elected on the basis of high academic achievement.[12]

Also, 'he was an important member of the debating team, and often represented Rutgers in inter-collegiate debates'. Doors had opened for Paul, but tragedy was to come.

'At the end of his junior year at college', said Eslanda, 'his beloved father died, on 17 May 1918 at the age of 73. Paul was heartbroken. Suddenly, he was without his great friend, his dear companion, his guiding spirit and inspiration. The blow saddened him in the midst of his youthful successes. He became quieter, more thoughtful, lonely. But the fine spirit of the father lived on for the son'.

'When he returned to Rutgers for his senior year, he worked harder than ever. When he graduated in June 1919, he had won his Phi Beta Kappa key, and had been selected by Walter Camp as end for his annual All-American football team; he was a "four-letter-man"', having 'won his "R" in four different sports'.[13]

End: a player who lines up at either end of the scrimmage, usually beside the tackles.

Tackle: a playing position in gridiron football.

Phi Beta Kappa key: the symbol of the Phi Beta Kappa society, a golden key engraved on the obverse with the image of a pointing finger, three stars, and the Greek letters from which the society takes its name.

Paul 'delivered the commencement oration; and he was elected to Cap and Skull.'[14]

'Commencement': a ceremony in which degrees or diplomas are conferred upon graduating students.

Commencement speech (oration): a speech made during the commencement.

Cap and Skull: a senior-year co-educational honor society at Rutgers University, founded on January 18, 1900. Admission to Cap and Skull is dependent on excellence in academics, athletics, the arts, and public service. Leadership as well as character are also considered crucial factors for membership.[15]

Continued Eslanda, 'It was extraordinarily significant of the boy's importance that he, a Negro, was chosen as one of the four most representative men in scholarship, athletics, and personality of that historic white university.'[16]

For Paul, another greatly satisfying event occurred. 'When he played his final game for Rutgers at commencement, a baseball match against Princeton, he was largely responsible for the Rutgers victory of 5-1. It was the first time in fifty years - since that first game in 1869 - that Rutgers had defeated Princeton in any branch of athletics.' However, 'the defeat of Princeton had a greater significance' for Paul 'than for his teammates. For them, it meant the defeat of a powerful rival; for him it meant the defeat of a long-hated institution'. And what made the victory particularly sweet was the fact that 'Generations of wealthy and aristocratic southerners [i.e. white, and from the southern states]' had attended Princeton, 'and southerners were 'notoriously prejudiced against Negroes'.[17]

Because the First World War (1914-1918) was in progress, no official All-American team was picked in that year of 1917.

In that year of 1917, Paul wrote a review of that year's football season. It was published in the *Rutgers Alumni Quarterly* 1918, and in it, he revealed his passion for, and gift of oratory. It began, 'The season of 1917 is over, but the memories thereof will fire the hearts of Rutgers men as long as football is football'.[18]

The First World War ended on 11 November 1918.

For the 1919 season, Paul was awarded twelve varsity letters in sports at Rutgers, including basketball, baseball, discus, shotput, and javelin as well as football.[19]

Letterman: in the US, a high school or college student who has reached a certain level of participation or performance as a member of a varsity team.

On 29 May 1919, Paul submitted his senior thesis. It was entitled, 'The Fourteenth Amendment, the Sleeping Giant of the American Constitution'.

14th Amendment: An amendment (1868) to the Constitution of the US that granted citizenship and equal civil and legal rights to African Americans and slaves who had been emancipated after the American Civil War, including them under the umbrella phrase 'All Persons Born or Naturalized in the United States'.[20] It was no accident that Paul had chosen this as his subject!

On 10 June 1919, Paul delivered the graduating class oration entitled, 'The New Idealism' at Rutgers 153rd Commencement.[21] He made the most of his opportunity!

'Today we feel that America has proved true to her trust. Realizing that there were worse things than war; that the liberties won through long years of travail were too sacred to be thrown away, though their continued possession entailed the last full measure of devotion, we paid again, in part, the price of liberty. In the fulfilment of our country's duty to civilisation, in its concentrating of all resources to the attainment of the ideal America, in the triumph of right over the forces of autocracy, we see the development of a new spirit, a new motive power in American life.'

Autocracy: a system of government by one person with absolute power; a country, state, or society governed in this way.[22]

'It will be the purpose of this new spirit to cherish and strengthen the heritage of freedom for which men have toiled, suffered, and died a thousand years; to prove that the possibilities of that larger freedom for which the noblest spirits have sacrificed their lives were no idle dreams; to give fuller expression to the principle upon which our national life is built. We realise that freedom is the most precious of our treasures, and it will not be allowed to vanish as long as men survive who offer their lives to keep it.'

'We know that neither institutions nor friends can make a race stand, unless it has strength in its own foundation; that races like individuals must stand or fall by their own merit; that to fully succeed they must practise their virtues of self-reliance, self-respect, industry, perseverance, and economy.'

'But, in order for us to successfully do all these things, it is necessary that you of the favoured race, catch a new vision and exemplify in your actions this new American spirit. That spirit which prompts you to compassion, a motive instinctive but cultivated and intensified by Christianity, embodying the desire to relieve the manifested distress of your fellows; that motive which realizes as the task of civilisation the achievement of happiness and the institution of community spirit.'[23] Paul's message to his white contemporaries was obvious!

Almost a decade later, on 22 September 1928, in an interview for *London Evening News and African World*, Paul recalled how, during his footballing days at Rutgers, he 'played American football and became pretty good. I remember that in a big match for my college the other side protested when I, a coloured man, walked on the field to play against them. The process did not worry me a lot, though, of course, it hurt. For all we coloured folk in America work with the heavy yoke of colour as a life load'.

'I played in that match and I played hard. I wasn't unnecessarily rough, but I was rough, and I handled some of their men absolutely without mercy. When it was over, I could have fainted with surprise. Every man in the enemy pack filed in front of me and shook my black hand!'[24]

Fifteen years later, on 3 December 1943, Paul made a plea for Negro baseball players to be included in the major leagues. 'When I played football at Rutgers, we met southern teams that threatened to cancel games if I was in the line-up. The games were played, and nothing happened. I was almost killed the first year, but I was accepted after I had proved my ability.' This latter statement was probably true on the first count, and definitely true on the second!

'I can understand the owners' fears that there would be trouble if Negroes were to play in the big leagues, but my football experience showed me such fears are groundless. Because baseball is a national game, it is up to baseball [i.e. the sport's governing body] to see that discrimination does not become the American pattern.'[25]

In February 1951, Paul once more, reflected on his mindset during his footballing days:

'When I was playing football, I had always to remember - whatever the provocation - that I represented a whole people. I had to play clean, and I did. Of course, once in a while the ambulance rolled up to take off one of the rough boys who had called me all the names in the book and slugged me every which way - but nobody ever saw me hit him. Of course, he was gone, but he somehow managed to fall right into my knee or my swinging elbow or fist. T'wasn't my fault. And I always help pick him up - so tenderly.'

'And in my classes I had to stay up late to prove that Negroes could also measure up in their studies. But every Negro boy and girl knows and accepts these obligations. We all know that we have a group responsibility.'[26]

For Paul to have achieved such distinction, both academically and on the sports field, was truly remarkable, if not unique!

1. Robeson, Paul, with Lloyd L. Brown, *Here I Stand*, p.24.
2. Ibid, p.25.
3. Robeson, Paul, Jr., *The Undiscovered Paul Robeson: An Artist's Journey,* 1898-1939, p.13.
4. Foner, Philip S., *Paul Robeson Speaks*, p.27.
5. Robeson, Paul, with Lloyd L. Brown, *Here I Stand*, op. cit., p.27.
6. Robeson, Eslanda Goode, *Paul Robeson: Negro,* pp.35-6.

7. Ibid, p.37.
8. Stevenson, A., and Waite, M., *Concise Oxford English Dictionary*.
9. Foner, Philip S., *Paul Robeson Speaks*, op. cit., p.154.
10. Stevenson, A., and Waite, M., *Concise Oxford English Dictionary*, op. cit.
11. Robeson, Eslanda Goode, *Paul Robeson: Negro,* p.39.
12. Stevenson, A., and Waite, M., *Concise Oxford English Dictionary*, op. cit.
13. Robeson, Eslanda Goode, *Paul Robeson: Negro,* op. cit., p.40.
14. Ibid, p.40.
15. *Wikipedia.*
16. Robeson, Eslanda Goode, *Paul Robeson: Negro,* op. cit., p.41.
17. Ibid, p.41.
18. Foner, Philip S., *Paul Robeson Speaks*, op. cit., p.49.
19. Ibid, p.28.
20. *Wikipedia.*
21. Foner, Philip S., *Paul Robeson Speaks*, op. cit., pp.27-8.
22. Stevenson, A., and Waite, M., *Concise Oxford English Dictionary*, op. cit.
23. Foner, Philip S., *Paul Robeson Speaks*, op. cit., pp.62-4.
24. Ibid, p.77.
25. Ibid, p.152.
26. Ibid, p.266.

CHAPTER 11

Harlem: Columbia University, New York City (1919-1923): Marriage to Eslanda (1921)

In July 1919, Paul relocated to Harlem, NYC. Said Eslanda, 'In 1919, Harlem had a complete life of its own. There were young and old Negro physicians and dentists, with much larger practices than they could comfortably look after themselves. Negroes owned beautiful houses and modern apartments; there were many fine churches; there were the YMCA and YWCA; there were several chapters of inter-collegiate fraternities and sororities; there were Negro graduates from the finest white universities in America; there were Negroes in every conceivable profession, business, and trade'.[1]

YMCA and YWCA: Young Men's and Young Women's Christian Associations.

Sororiety: a society for female students in a university or college.[2]

Paul 'naturally settled in Harlem' said Eslanda. Here, he soon found himself among friends. Many children with whom he had grown up in New Jersey had come to New York to find work, or to attend schools. Many athletes with, and against whom he had played while at Rutgers, were now in New York. Many people interested in athletics had read of his prowess on the gridiron and in other sports, and many had seen him in action'.

'The Negroes especially, knew all about him and were very proud of the fine record he had made at Rutgers, both in scholarship and athletics. Paul Robeson was a hero: he fulfilled the ideal of nearly every class of Negro. Those who admired intellect pointed to his Phi Beta Kappa key; those who admired physical prowess talked about his remarkable record. His simplicity and charm were captivating.'

Furthermore, 'everyone was glad that he was so typically Negroid in appearance, colour, and features; everyone was glad that he was taking up the dignified profession of the law. He soon became Harlem's special favourite and is so, still. Everyone knew, admired, and liked him; he was affectionately but respectfully, known as "Paul" or "Robey". His unaffected friendliness, his natural tact, his great gift for "mixing", his real interest in everyone, soon made him "one of the boys"'.[3]

'He could always be counted upon to referee a game of basketball for the Parish House [perhaps organized under the auspices of the local pastor] or the YMCA. He could even be counted upon to coach a team or play in a team. He could be depended upon to sing bass in the church choir on Sunday mornings. He would "speak" or sing a solo or two at the local concerts to help fill out the programme. He was a member of two popular fraternities: one inter-collegiate and one professional. He was a welcome addition to any social gathering because he was a good dancer, a good "mixer", was liked by everyone, and could be depended upon to make himself pleasant to other guests.'[4]

In 1920, Paul entered Columbia University's Law School; in his spare time 'working at odd jobs and playing some professional football to earn tuition money'.[5]

At Columbia, said Eslanda, Paul 'was immediately commandeered to play in the Law School basketball and other teams. He made friends easily and soon became part of campus life - so much a part of it that, when the graduating class of the university held its annual senior dinner at the Hotel Astor in 1920, he was guest of honour at the speaker's table. R. L. Condon, the president of the class, who sat at Paul's right, said that "Robeson was invited by the whole class because he was one of Columbia's most brilliant men". Paul was as thoroughly comfortable at Columbia among his white classmates as he was in Harlem among his Negro friends'.[6]

In that year of 1920, Paul made his acting debut at the Harlem YMCA with the Provincetown Players, having the leading role in *Simon the Cyrenian*, one of *Plays for a Negro Theater* by white US poet and playwright, (Frederic) Ridgley Torrence (1874-1950).[7]

In 1921, Paul married Eslanda Cardozo Goode, who was studying chemistry at Columbia and was 'soon to become the first black woman to head a pathology laboratory'.[8]

On 4 April 1922, Paul made his Broadway debut in *Taboo*, a drama set in Africa. In July, Paul visited England to appear in a production of *Taboo* (renamed *Voodoo*) with British stage actress, Mrs Patrick Campbell.[9]

It was in London that Paul first met black US musician, Lawrence Brown, who had come to Europe to accompany black US tenor, Roland Hayes.

Lawrence ('Larry') Benjamin Brown (1893-1972): US singer, composer, pianist, and arranger of African American folk songs.

Larry Brown would subsequently become Paul's accompanist, in what was to become an immensely fruitful association.

Paul wrote very little about his early days in Harlem but fortunately, Eslanda has proved to be a great chronicler of the events of his life. The attraction of Harlem for Paul, as she explained eloquently, was that this was 'a coloured community. One knows, without being told, that the white person occasionally seen in the streets of Harlem does not really *belong* there; that he is merely there on some errand of business or is passing through to some place beyond. Only Negroes *belong* in Harlem, and they actively resent the presence of white tourists'.[10]

In Harlem, US singers Ethel Waters, Bessie Smith, Mamie Smith, and Clara Smith, performed at the 'Negro theater'. They sang 'some raw, rich, haunting "Blues"', in 'deep, husky' voices.

'Blues': melancholy music of black American folk origin.[11]

There were also night clubs for Negroes.[12] Said Eslanda, 'Harlem belongs to all American Negroes. It is the place they can call home; it is a place where they *belong*'.[13]

Furthermore, Harlem was where one met one's friends. 'It is almost impossible for a Negro, no matter from what part of America he comes, to stroll down Seventh Avenue late on a sunny afternoon and not see someone from his home town - or at least someone who knows someone he knows. Negroes from all states in the Union come to Harlem to live and work and study, because conditions are better, opportunities greater, and the schools and universities finer than those in their home cities.'[14]

At the YMCA or YWCA, a Negro meets 'young Negroes from all parts of the world. Here, there are inter-collegiate fraternities and sororities, and other college and social clubs. There are educational, social, political, and philanthropic organizations, all made up of, and entirely run by and for, Negroes. There are innumerable public and private dining-rooms and restaurants where a Negro is an expected and welcome guest. A Negro knows exactly where he is in Harlem: he is among friends; he is at home'.[15]

Did Whites have any place at all in Harlem? Said Eslanda, 'the white visitors to Harlem were at first surprised to find the Negro social functions not unlike their own - perhaps a little more colourful; that Negro homes were somewhat like their own; that the Negro host and hostess had seen the same good plays, read the same good books, and heard the same operas and concerts they had; that perhaps even their sons and daughters were attending the same universities'.

It was Eslanda's opinion that 'this "mixing" is the best thing that could happen to help solve the Negro problem in America. When white people come to know the Negro as he really is, whether or not they decide to like him, become bosom friends with him, or marry him, the greatest single barrier will be broken down'.[16]

Paul's younger brother, Ezekiel died on 24 July 1922.

In the spring of 1923, Paul graduated from Columbia Law School and applied to law firms for work. Meanwhile, he worked as a singer 'in Harlem's famed "Cotton Club"'.[17]

1. Robeson, Eslanda Goode, *Paul Robeson: Negro,* p.67.
2. Stevenson, A., and Waite, M., *Concise Oxford English Dictionary.*
3. Robeson, Eslanda Goode, *Paul Robeson: Negro,* op. cit., pp.67-8
4. Ibid, pp.68-9.
5. Foner, Philip S., *Paul Robeson Speaks*, p.28.
6. Robeson, Eslanda Goode, *Paul Robeson: Negro,* op. cit., pp.68-9.
7. Foner, Philip S., *Paul Robeson Speaks*, op. cit., p.28.
8. Ibid, p.28.
9. Ibid, p.28.
10. Robeson, Eslanda Goode, *Paul Robeson: Negro,* op. cit., p.47
11. Stevenson, A., and Waite, M., *Concise Oxford English Dictionary,* op. cit.
12. Robeson, Eslanda Goode, *Paul Robeson: Negro,* op. cit., p.48.
13. Ibid, p.48.
14. Ibid, p.50.
15. Ibid, p.50-1.
16. Ibid, pp.57-8.
17. Foner, Philip S., *Paul Robeson Speaks*, op. cit., p.28.

CHAPTER 12

Eslanda's Background

Eslanda Cardozo Goode was born in Washington, DC on 15 December 1895. Her father, John Jacob Astor Goode (1863-1901), from Chicago, was of Native American, English, and Scottish ancestry. John 'became a clerk in the War Department by winning first place among 500 candidates in a competitive examination. Later, he completed his study of law at Howard University in the evenings'.[1]

Eslanda's mother, Eslanda Elbert Cardozo from Washington DC was of Spanish, Jewish, and African-American (slave) ancestry.

John died when Eslanda was only 4 years old, leaving the family with little savings. Her mother and namesake, Eslanda responded to this crisis by teaching herself beauty culture and building up a thriving beauty-care business located to top-level white society women, as well as to wealthy Blacks. Although Mrs Goode never became rich, the family lived well by the standards of their times, and money was available for the children's education.'[2]

Eslanda 'finished high school at 16 and won a four-year scholarship to the University of Illinois, ranking third in a state-sponsored competitive examination. There, she majored in chemistry'.[3] In her senior year, Eslanda transferred to Columbia University, New York, from where she graduated in chemistry. 'She first became politically active during her years at Columbia, when her own interest in racial equality was reinforced by young intellectuals in New York. When then, she started to work at New York-Presbyterian Hospital, she soon became the head histological chemist of surgical pathology: the first black person to hold such a position.'

'In 1920, both Essie and Paul attended summer school at Columbia: Paul for law courses and Essie for a course in preparation for Columbia Medical School in the fall.'[4] As already mentioned, they married one year later, in August 1921. Meanwhile, Eslanda gave up her intentions to study medicine in order to support her husband Paul as his business manager.

1. Robeson, Paul, Jr., *The Undiscovered Paul Robeson: An Artist's Journey,* 1898-1939, p.47.
2. Ibid, p.47.
3. Ibid, p.48.
4. Ibid, p.48.

CHAPTER 13

The Theatre and Concerts: Paul junior is born (2 November 1927)

After Columbia University, what next for Paul? Said Eslanda, 'A very successful and socially prominent lawyer' who was an alumnus and also a trustee of Rutgers University, 'invited Paul to come into the office of his firm to work'. This was Louis William Stotesbury of the law firm, Stotesbury & Minter of NYC. 'The offer was doubly welcome to Paul, because it was almost impossible for a young Negro lawyer to acquire any experience in big legal work.'[1]

'Paul enjoyed the work.' However eventually, the clerks and other members of the firm objected to the constant presence of so conspicuous a Negro in the office, and Paul felt forced to withdraw.[2] In fact, 'a secretary refused to take dictation from him'.[3]

Paul, said Lloyd L. Brown, 'wasn't interested in joining a profession in which he couldn't reach the highest rungs'.[4] He therefore, 'returned to Harlem', but was 'uncertain as to what he should do next'.[5] An opportunity came when he was offered lead roles with Provincetown Players (a theatre company that originated in Provincetown, Massachusetts) in not one, but two plays by US playwright, Eugene O'Neill. Both plays were staged in 1924 at the Provincetown Playhouse, Manhattan. The first was *All God's Chillun Got Wings* (1924), in which he played 'Jim Harris'. Here, the theme is one of interracial love. The second, was a revival of *The Emperor Jones* (1925) in which he played 'Brutus Jones'. Here, the theme is racism.[6]

On 5 May 1924, Paul was threatened by the Ku Klux Klan: an extreme white supremacy secret society in the USA, because in his role in *All God's Chillun Got Wings*, 'a white woman would kiss his hand'.[7]

Over two decades later, Paul made a speech which was broadcast by the Mutual Broadcasting System (commercial radio network). In it, with reference to the American Crusade to End Lynching he said, 'People of America, we appeal to you to help wipe out this inhuman bestiality, this Ku Klux Klan-hooded violence'.[8]

The American Crusade against Lynching: an organization created in 1946 and headed by Paul Robeson, dedicated to eliminating lynching in the US.

Lynch: in which a group of people kill someone for an alleged offence without a legal trial, especially by hanging.[9]

Paul was not to be intimidated. *All God's Chillun Got Wings* opened on 15 May 1924, and it 'was an immediate success'.[10] *The Emperor Jones* opened in 1925. In fact, so pleased was Eugene O'Neill with Paul's performance in both plays that he presented him with a 'book containing his plays', on the flyleaf of which he wrote, 'In gratitude to Paul Robeson, in whose interpretation of Brutus Jones I have found the most complete satisfaction an author can get - that of seeing his creation born into flesh and blood'.[11]

Said Paul, if he could make his audience 'realise fully the pitiful struggle of Jim Harris and reduce them to tears for him at the end - weeping because a Negro has suffered - I will have done something to make them realise, even if only subconsciously and for a few moments, that Negroes are the same kind of people they themselves are; suffer as they suffer, weep as they weep; that all this arbitrary separation because of colour is unimportant - that we are all human beings'.[12]

Said Eslanda of Paul, 'his step from the theatre into the concert hall was a natural one; his friends, and even the critics who had reviewed his performances, had long admired and spoken enthusiastically about his beautiful voice. So, when after long months of enforced idleness because there were no suitable plays in which he could act, someone suggested that he give a concert of his Negro music in conjunction with Lawrence Brown. This suggestion received immediate and important support from all his wide circle of friends'.[13]

The concert was performed on 19 April 1925 at the Greenwich Village Theatre, NYC. It was 'made up solely of Negro music - three groups of spirituals and one group of secular and dialect songs'. The concert 'was a resounding success', and it brought Negro Spirituals to a 'prominent place in music in [the] music world'.[14] Said Eslanda, 'At the end of the programme the entire audience remained seated, clamouring for more'. Paul and Brown 'gave many encores, and finally, tired out, could only bow and smile their appreciation to the still applauding audience. It was a memorable evening'.[15]

A second concert followed, on 3 May 1925. Whereupon, 'an enterprising concert manager promptly signed Paul and "Larry" [Lawrence] for an extensive concert tour for the following year'.[16] This was concert producer and agent, James B. Pond. Paul once declared that 'All men are brothers because of their music'.[17]

From now on, Brown frequently accompanied Paul, performing on the piano and singing harmony. Filmed recordings of the pair indicate that between Paul and Brown, there was real affection. One clip, for example, shows them play-boxing together.[18]

On 11 September 1925, *The Emperor Jones* opened in in London 'to critical acclaim', with Paul in the leading role.[19] Her husband 'felt even more at home in London than he had in America', said Eslanda. 'He learned to love the great stretches of parks and the quiet squares in the heart of the city. He strolled along the Embankment by the hour gazing at the river; he became an enthusiast about cricket, and many warm, sunny days found him sitting lazily at stands at Lord's, or at the Oval [London cricket grounds] watching and enjoying the test matches'.

'There were fewer inconveniences for him as a Negro in London. He did not have to live in a segregated district; he leased a charming flat in Chelsea near his friends; he dined at The Ivy (a delightful restaurant with marvellous food, directly across from the theatre where he was playing). He ate at many other restaurants in town with his white or coloured friends, without fear of discrimination which all Negroes encountered in America. He was a welcome guest in hotels at the seaside places where he spent many week-ends.'[20]

Disappointingly, however, *The Emperor Jones* 'had an unexpectedly short run in London. Everyone had hoped that it would run into December 1925 and Paul was greatly disappointed when it closed early, in October. The London critics and public had given him a remarkably warm personal reception, but they did not like the play'.[21] Nevertheless, the Robesons 'remained in London for a month, enjoying the theatre, concerts, and their friends. Then, as the bad weather set in, they left for the Riviera in search of sunshine'.[22]

On 20 November 1925, Paul's beloved brother, William ('Bill') died.

Paul returned to the USA, and on 5 January 1926 launched 'his first concert tour, in which, as always, he had Lawrence Brown as his associate'. Having been reunited with his friends in Harlem, 'he settled down to work. He sang in New York and in many other large cities, with great success'.[23]

On 25 January 1926, Paul and Brown made their first RCA Victor (US record label) recording, of the love song 'L'il Gal' by Black US poet, Paul L. Dunbar; music composed by Black US Composer and singer, J. Rosamond Johnson. It quickly sold 50,000 copies.[24]

> 'Oh, de weathah it is balmy an' de breeze is sighin' low.
> Li'l' gal,
> An' de mockin' bird is singin' in de locus' by de do',
> Li'l' gal;
> Dere 's a hummin' an' a bummin' in de lan' f'om eas' to wes',
> I 's a–sighin' fu' you, honey, an' I nevah know no res'.
> Fu' dey 's lots o' trouble brewin' an' a–stewin' in my breas',
> Li'l' gal.'

On 2 November 1927, Paul and Eslanda's son, Paul Leroy Bustill Robeson (Paul junior, or 'Pauli') was born. Said Eslanda, 'he was an exact replica of his father; the likeness was so startling that it became a joke amongst their friends. Even his baby voice was deep. No one ever asked his name; everyone simply and naturally, called him Paul'.[25]

Many years later, Paul junior would say of his father, 'I can honestly say, for me, that yes, there were downsides overall, but I wouldn't trade him for anybody in the universe'.[26]

1. Robeson, Eslanda Goode, *Paul Robeson: Negro,* p.70.
2. Ibid, p.71.
3. Foner, Philip S., *Paul Robeson Speaks*, p.28.
4. *'Paul Robeson: Here I Stand', PBS American Masters, 1999.
5. Robeson, Eslanda Goode, *Paul Robeson: Negro,* op. cit., p.72.
6. Foner, Philip S., *Paul Robeson Speaks*, op. cit., p.28.
7. Ibid, p.28.
8. Ibid, p.177.
9. Stevenson, A., and Waite, M., *Concise Oxford English Dictionary.*
10. Foner, Philip S., *Paul Robeson Speaks*, op. cit., p.28.
11. Robeson, Eslanda Goode, *Paul Robeson: Negro,* op. cit., p.79.
12. Ibid, p.85.
13. Ibid, p.87.
14. Foner, Philip S., *Paul Robeson Speaks*, op. cit., p.29.
15. Robeson, Eslanda Goode, *Paul Robeson: Negro,* op. cit., p.89.
16. Ibid, p.90.
17. *'Paul Robeson: Here I Stand', PBS American Masters, 1999.

18. Ibid.
19. Foner, Philip S., *Paul Robeson Speaks*, op. cit., p.29.
20. Robeson, Eslanda Goode, *Paul Robeson: Negro,* op. cit., pp.96-7.
21. Ibid, p.97.
22. Ibid, p.98.
23. Ibid, p.107.
24. *'Paul Robeson: Here I Stand', PBS American Masters, 1999.
25. Robeson, Eslanda Goode, *Paul Robeson: Negro,* op. cit., p.118.
26. *'Paul Robeson: Here I Stand', PBS American Masters, 1999.

CHAPTER 14

How Eslanda Helped Her Husband, Paul

In her biography of her husband, Eslanda explained how she encouraged Paul to perfect his art as a singer.

It was in Boston, Massachusetts in November 1924 that Paul had given his first professional recital. However, prior to a performance that he subsequently gave in Boston, he 'caught a cold in the draughty train' after 'a wretched overnight train ride from New York'.[1]

Said Paul to his accompanist Lawrence ('Larry') Brown, 'I haven't any voice at all. My throat's tied up in a knot, and I can't possibly sing a note. I think the only fair thing to do is to go out and tell the audience that I'm sorry, but I must disappoint them; they will see for themselves that I have a dreadful cold. And I will pay the full expense of the concert'. Paul 'was ready to cry', said Eslanda. However, despite this major setback, Eslanda and Larry encouraged Paul to go on stage anyway. Said she, 'Paul was so frightened that he walked on the stage in a trance. He never sang so badly in his life. His rich, lovely voice was tight and hard and unrecognisable'.

The outcome was, that although 'the audience was a little embarrassed ... something of Paul's tenseness and deep sincerity got through to them, and they appreciated that'. As for Paul, 'Boston was his home ground, and he had so wanted to do well there'. In fact, he 'was so shocked at his performance that he declared he would never sing again. He would return to the stage [as an actor] and remain there. Poor boy, his despair was pathetic'.

Mercifully, continued Eslanda, 'the newspapers next day were amazingly kind, nearly all of them mentioning the obvious cold'. But the couple 'returned to New York greatly discouraged'.

Eslanda gave the matter some thought. She asked herself, how was it 'that Paul's voice could be so gorgeous one day and so dead the next?' And how was it that when 'other concert singers had the same sort of difficulties to combat ... they managed to sing fairly well in spite of such things. Why couldn't Paul? There must be some way to sing well, at least fairly well, over a cold; there must be a way to sing well even over nervousness; there must be some general fortification against these enemies of the voice'.

Eslanda came to the conclusion that voice training was the answer, and she 'began looking for a vocal teacher'. But this 'must be no ordinary teacher'. The person would have to be someone who 'would listen to him sing, and when he sang well point out to him how he sang, and show him how he might always accomplish this, even under unfavourable circumstances. Paul had no knowledge of singing technique. He had one of those naturally beautiful and perfectly placed voices which only went wrong when he was nervous or had a cold. He had no idea how he sang; he just opened up his throat and his heart, and, if all was well, he sang divinely. Essie wanted to find a teacher who would not touch his voice as such; it seemed to her quite perfect. The more recitals [by her husband] she heard, the more prejudiced she became against the so-called "trained" voice. The technique seemed to level all the voices to one uninteresting mould'.

It seemed to Eslanda, 'that the more perfectly, technically, one sang, the less interesting the voice became' It was her opinion that such a 'trained voice' would lose 'all the colour, roundness and personality which distinguish voices individually. She didn't want Paul's voice to sink to this mould'.

By coincidence, said Eslanda, Teresa Armitage came to New York, 'and the Robesons' proverbial good luck brought them together'. In fact, Teresa was something of a tour de force in the world of music. She was the author of several music books for students, and of several music manuals for teachers. From 1908 to 1929 she was Series Editor of the *Laurel Music Series*, published by C. C. Birchard of Boston.

Eslanda continued, 'Teresa Armitage had taught singing in the high schools in Chicago when Essie had been a student there. She had admired the little girl's rich contralto voice and had advised her to become a singer; she had even given her vocal lessons for a year, and during the year they had become firm friends'. Teresa was also the author of several books on musical instruction.

'Miss Armitage was delighted to see "Eslanda" again (she was the only person who ever called Essie by her full name) and was curious and eager to learn what she had done with her voice. Essie explained that she had done nothing with it, but had been rather successful with her chemistry.'

Eslanda had been the first histological chemist of surgical pathology at the New York Presbyterian Hospital.

'"But", she said enthusiastically, "I've married the most beautiful voice I've ever heard, and I want you to help me with it". Teresa, said Eslanda, 'had worked out a system of her own, based upon natural vocal principles for the individual'. Furthermore, said Eslanda, Teresa 'was also something of a psychologist, and had an uncanny accuracy in sensing what was wrong with a singer mentally, physically, and vocally. She was the ideal person for Paul'.

As Teresa was so busy with her own musical commitments, however, she subsequently introduced Paul to another teacher, Frantz Proschowsky, 'but there came a time when Paul seemed to make no further progress'. However, by another 'fortunate coincidence', he was thrown 'into the arms of another musical friend [unidentified] who suggested that he study with a famous German voice teacher [unidentified] who divided her time between New York and Berlin. Paul went to her and learned a great deal more; she helped him enormously, but just as they were making real progress, she left for her Berlin season'.

Within a month, however, Teresa returned to New York on a permanent basis, where she 'congratulated him upon his splendid progress, and undertook the task of continuing his musical education herself. She has always remained his great friend and vocal adviser'.

When Paul expressed anxiety that the range of his voice was too limited, Teresa was swift to correct him: 'Now, my dear child, that low note you just sang so beautifully was low D, and the last magnificent top note was middle E. You just think your range is short. It's all of two and a quarter octaves, which is long enough for any reasonable person'. At such good news, Paul 'grinned, and danced up and down in his delight'.

Teresa instructed him as follows: 'Now, Paul, *don't dig* for your low notes, raise your chin and sing them freely; *think* them high, and they will be bright; if you keep reaching down for them they will be dark. You *must not* climb up and reach for that top note; think it low and bring your chin down on it, and it will come easily'.

'When you set your throat and cover your tones, you tire the muscles', said Teresa. The secret was, she said, to relax his throat. Whereupon 'you will find the more you sing the more flexible your voice will be, because correct singing oils the chords naturally and rests the voice'.

'And, sure enough, to his amazement, his low notes became clear and resonant, and his high notes easy and firm. Paul was elated. "It's all so simple", he said.'

'"Don't *set* your throat - that closes it", Miss Armitage continued. "Relax it, and you'll see how the voice rolls out". Paul tried relaxing his throat, and his whole body as well. "Gee", he said delightedly, after an hour's work, "you know my throat doesn't feel tired at all; in fact, my voice actually feels rested". He strolled up and down the studio, amazed that this should be so. Miss Armitage laughed. "And now, my child, you will always know that you are singing *right* when you do not tire".'

The outcome was, said Eslanda, that 'Paul was tremendously interested, and worked long and faithfully'.[2]

1. Robeson, Eslanda Goode, *Paul Robeson: Negro,* p.109.
2. Ibid, pp.109-114.

0a Preface The Author with his great-grandmother Jane Benwell – 'Nan', both great admirers of Paul Robeson!
Photo: Jean Norman.

0b Preface His Master's Voice, gramophone record, 'Water Boy', 78 rpm speed, Paul Robeson arranged by A. Robinson. Bass in English with piano.

0c Preface The Author's parents, Jean (née Waldin) and Christopher ('Chris') Norman on their wedding day, 25 March 1940. Photo: Jean Norman.

*0d Preface Thomas ('Tom') Waldin, his wife Esther (née Benwell), and their daughter Jean.
Photo: Jean Norman.*

*0e Preface end
The Author's wife
Rachel with her fathe[r]
Arthur E. Jordan,
8 April 2005.*

2 Reverend William Drew Robeson, father of Paul Robeson.
Photo: Joyce Mosley.

3a Maria Louisa Robeson (née Bustill), mother of Paul Robeson. Photo: Joyce Mosley.

3b 127th Regiment United States Colored Troops battle flag, painted by David Bustill Bowser. Photo: Morphy Auctions.

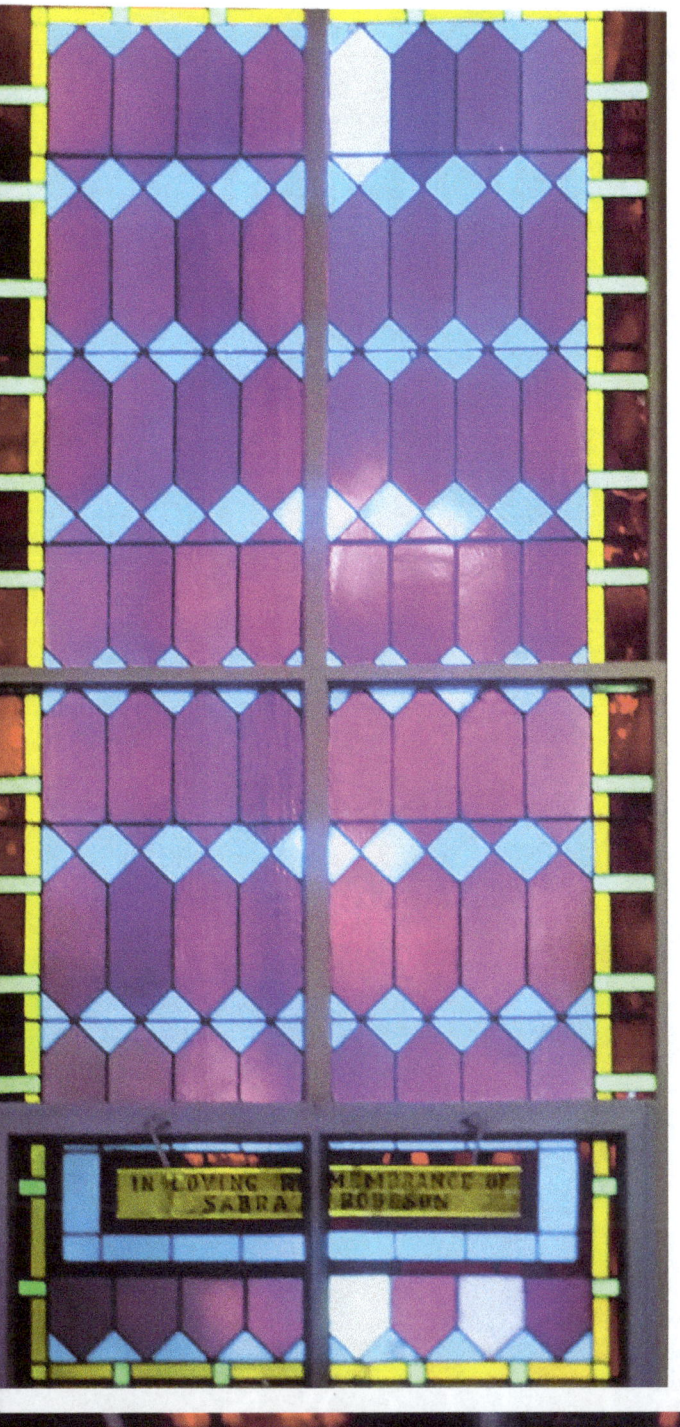

4a A stained-glass window in Witherspoon Street Presbyterian church, Princeton, New Jersey, inscribed "In Loving Remembrance of Sabra Robeson", installed by Rev William D. Robeson, pastor, in memory of his slave-born mother.

Photo;
courtesy of Denyse Leslie.

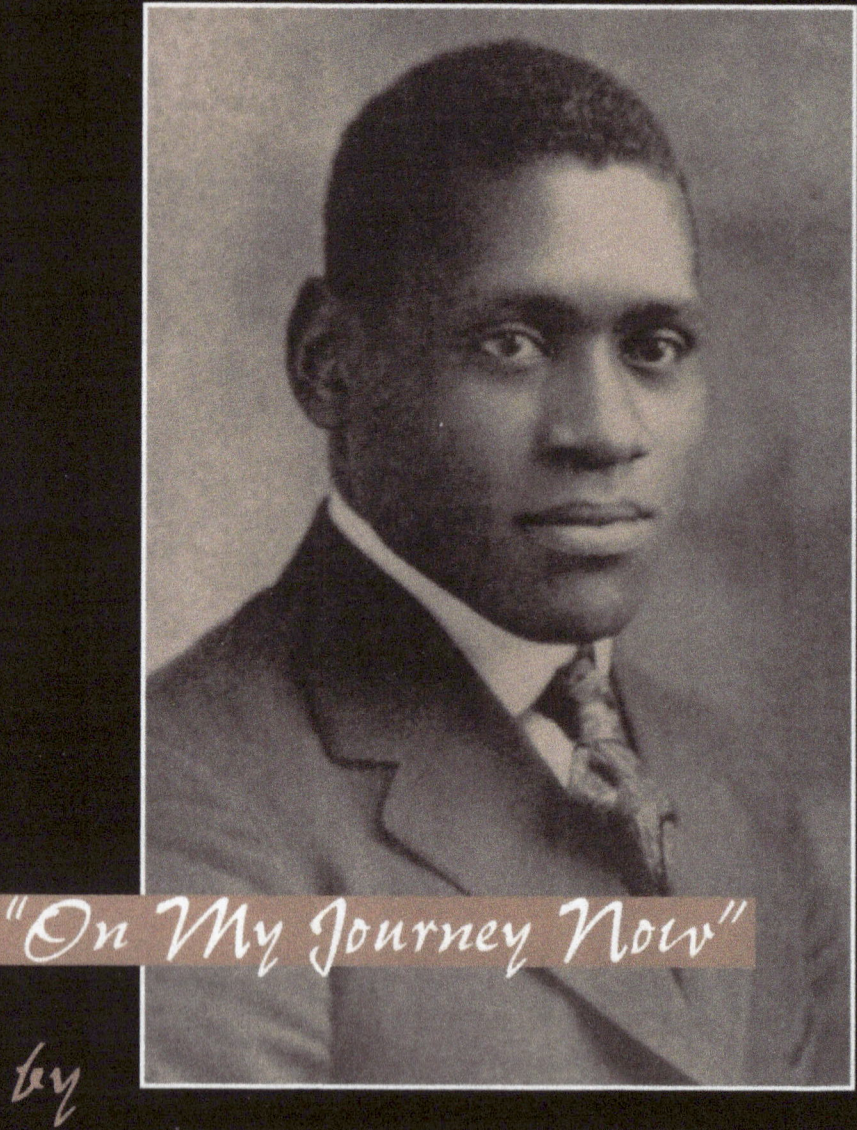

9 *The Young Paul Robeson* by Lloyd L. Brown. (Book cover)

a Paul Robeson: All-American Rutgers end, 1919, unknown author, Wikimedia Commons.

14 Music book by Paul Robeson's voice coach Teresa Armitage.

*10b Grave of William Drew Robeson and his wife Maria Louisa née Bustill.
Photo: Princeton Cemetery.*

16a Paul Robeson and US operatic soprano Ruby Pearl Elzy in The Emperor Jones, *1933. Photo: DVD Beaver. Wikimedia Commons.*

16b Paul Robeson as 'Othello' and German-US actress Uta Thyra Hagen as 'Desdemona', Othello, Broadway, 1933-4.
Photo: US Library of Congress.
Wikimedia Commons.

16c Paul Robeson and Hungarian actress Ágay Irén in Sanders of the River, London, 1934. Unknown photographer. Wikimedia Commons.

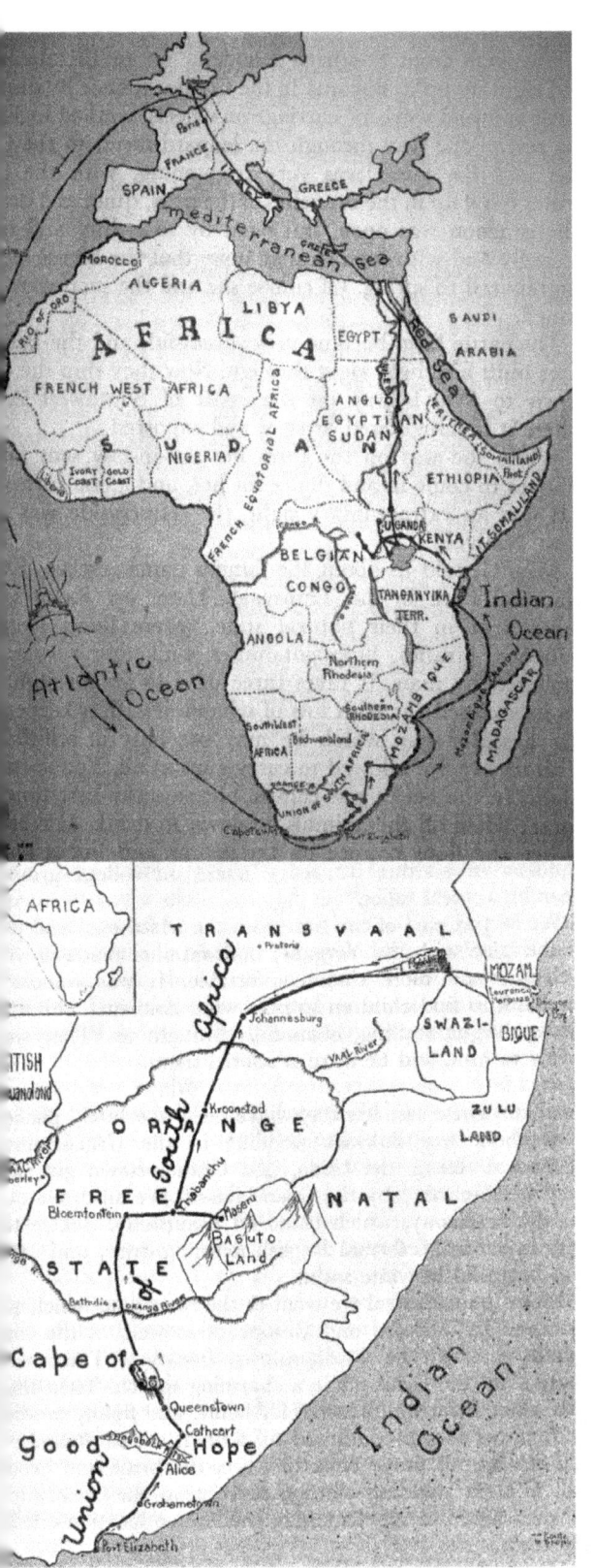

17a Eslanda's African Journey: London to Southern Africa. From African Journey.

17b Eslanda's African Journey: from The Cape to the Transvaal. From African Journey.

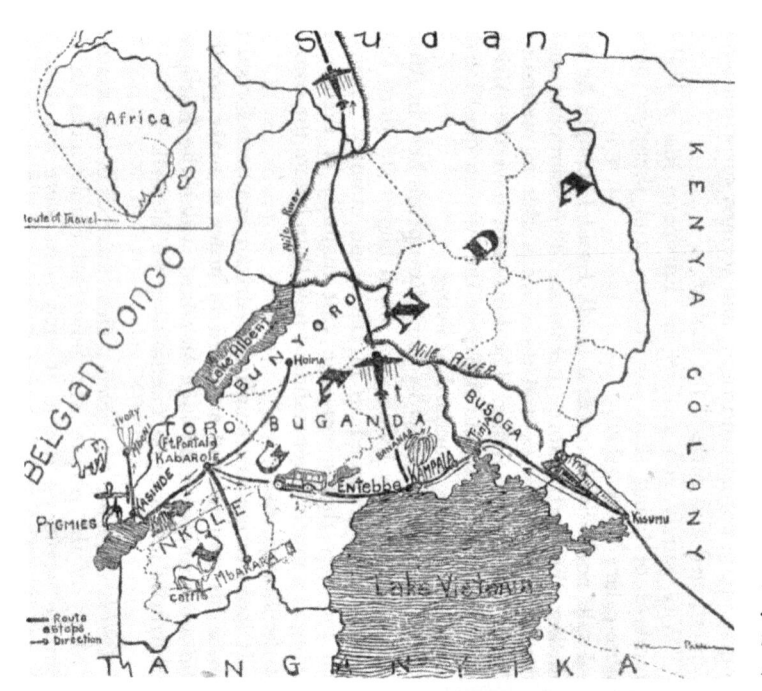

17c Eslanda's African Journey: from Kenya to the Congo and Sudan. From African Journey.

19a Composer Earl Robinson and Paul Robeson at a rehearsal for the first performance of Robinson's 'Ballad for Americans', c. November 1939. Photo: CBS. Wikimedia Commons.

*b (Left to Right) New Zealander David Jenkins (host); Mrs Eleanor Roosevelt (America's Frist .dy); Paul Robeson; US music critic Deems Taylor; The Hon. Walter Nash, New Zealand's Minister the US as that country's diplomatic representative; George Palmer, Superintendent in charge of .aintaining the Statue of Liberty (the foundation stone of which was laid on 5 August 1884). .ice of America radio programme, c.1942. Photo: Sir Walter Nash Collection. Wikimedia Commons.

*c Paul Robeson and Puerto Rican actor and film director José Ferrer, watching softball with other .embers of the cast of Othello, Central Park, New York City, c. 1943 or 1944. .oto: Library of Congress. Wikimedia Commons.

19d Image of Paul Robeson used in the advertisement for the Columbia Masterworks Records release of Othello, 19 February 1945. Photo: Life magazine. Wikimedia Commons.

20 Jackie Robinson, Brooklyn Dodgers, 1954. Photo: Bob Sandberg, Look magazine and Cowles Communications. Wikimedia Commons.

23 Paul Robeson with US educator, publisher, and civil rights activist Charlotta Bass, both of whom were accused of disloyalty by the HUAC. Photo: LA Times Photographic Archive, UCLA Library, c. 1949. Wikimedia Commons.

25 Paul Robeson on stage at the National Eisteddfod of Wales, Ebbw Vale, 1958.
Photo: Geof Charles.
Wikimedia Commons.

27 Grave of Eslanda Goode Robeson, Ferncliff Cemetery, Hartsdale, Westchester County, New York. Photo: David Zipperer.

30 Benjamin Congleton' marriage licence application, 31 May 1889. Ancestry.

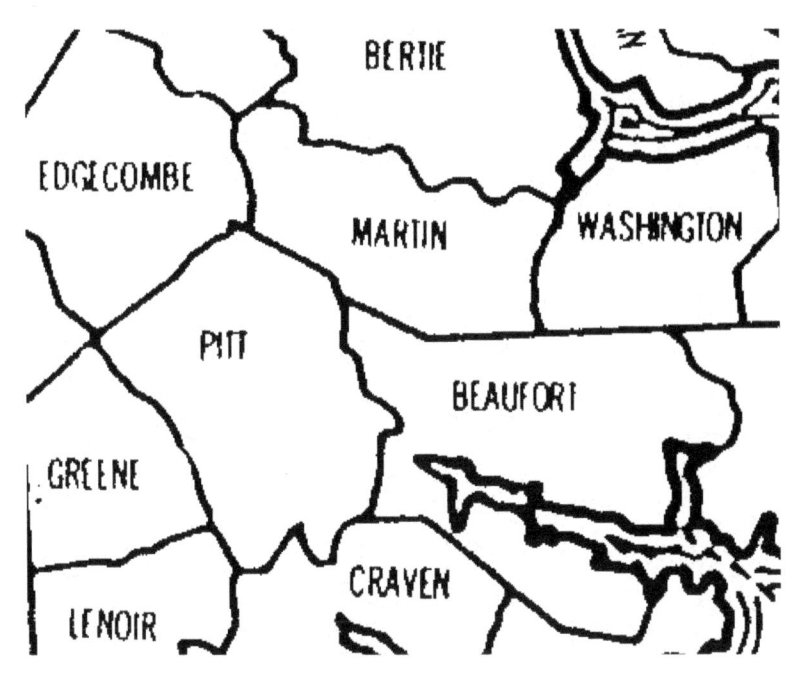

32a Relationship of Martin, Pitt, and Beaufort Counties, North Carolina. Photo: University of North Carolina Library.

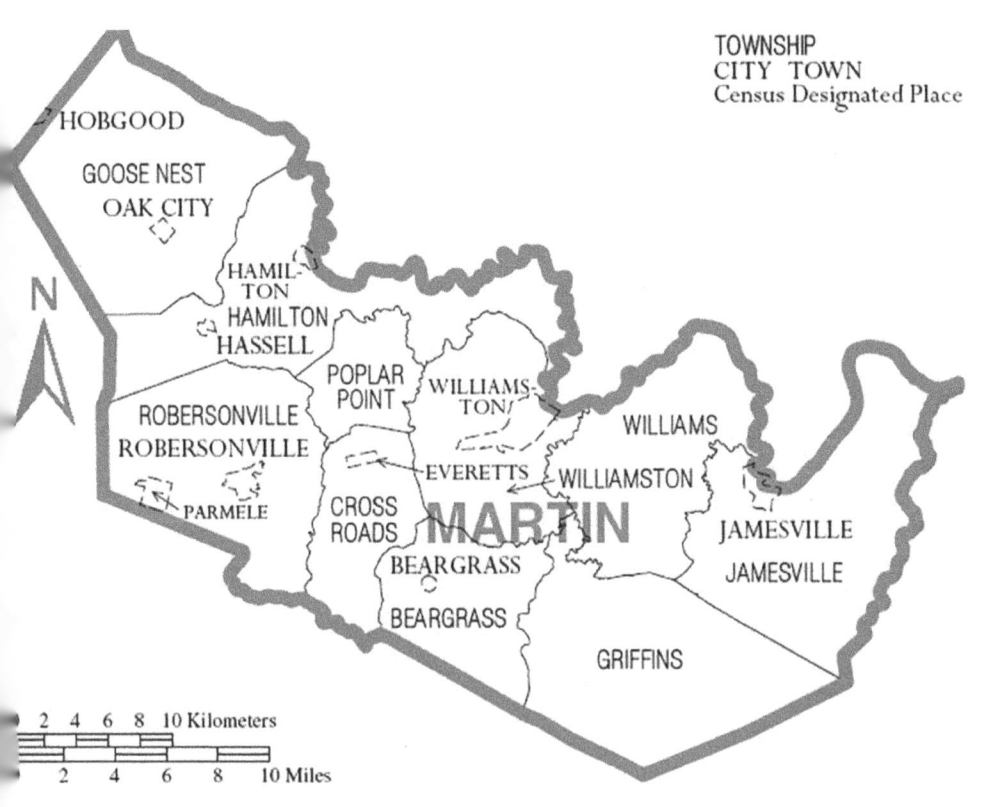

32b Map of Martin County, North Carolina showing municipalities and towns. Photo: US Census website.

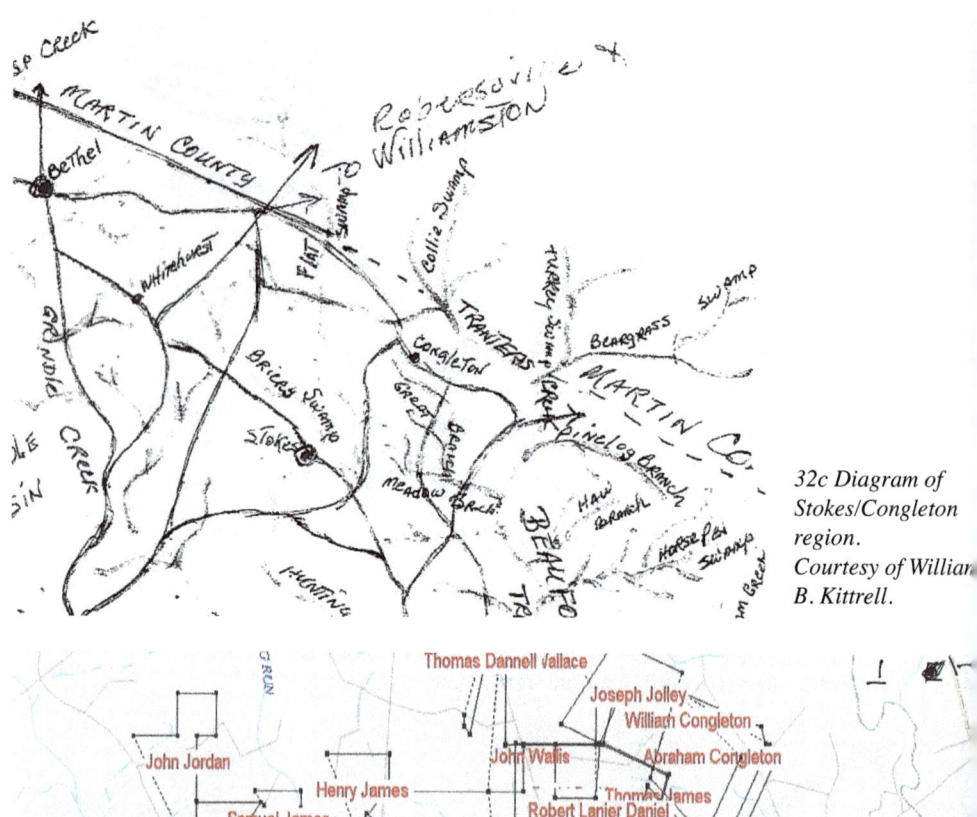

32c Diagram of Stokes/Congleton region.
Courtesy of William B. Kittrell.

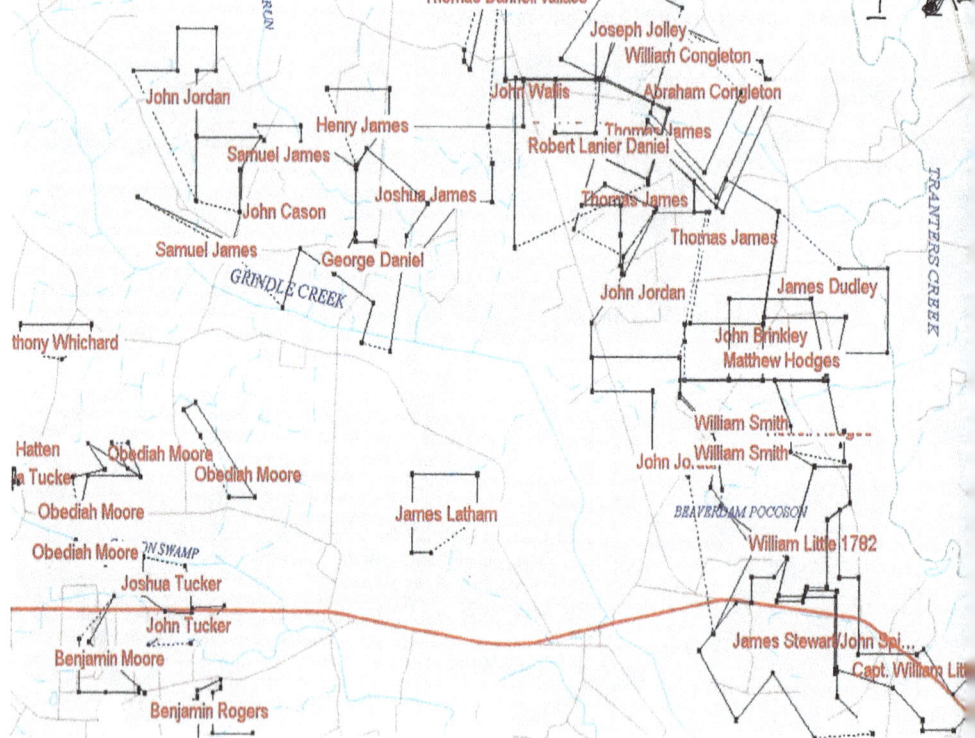

32d Land owned by Congletons, Pitt County Deed Map, 1773.
Courtesy of William B. Kittrell.

CHAPTER 15

Paul's Alleged Faults

Said Eslanda to Paul, 'Suppose you tell Martha some of your faults. She's as sure as you are that you have them. Come on, trot them out'.

'Martha Sampson': a pseudonym that Eslanda used for 'one of the old crowd Paul had been fortunate enough to find again in London'.[1]

Said Paul of his wife, 'she thinks I'm brave and honest and moral, when, as a matter of fact, I'm none of those things. Take courage, for instance. I think I'm a coward. Why, I can remember time after time in my football career when I could have and should have made fine plays [manoeuvres] in a pinch, I welched them because I knew I'd get hurt'.

Pinch: a critical point in the game.[2]

Welch: fail to honour and obligation.[3]

What about honesty? 'Yes, I'm dishonest too', said Paul. 'There was the money Dad [his father William Drew] used to send me at college. I knew he was old and tired, and that the money came hard, and that he wanted me to use it for important things, but I spent it on things he wouldn't have approved of, or threw it away on trifles; and then lied to him about it. That was low dishonesty.'

Paul also referred to loans that he had received from his brother, Ben which were intended to be used 'to pay important bills and family debts. I knew the bills and the debts were not particularly urgent, so I occasionally kept a cheque and spent it for myself'. Furthermore, said Paul, he had often spent money that he and Eslanda could not afford, 'and I'm not even honest enough to tell her I took the money'.

Here, Eslanda sprang to her husband's defence. 'But Martha', she said, 'if he wasn't essentially honest, would these things worry him so? He has stewed so over his brother's money during the last few years, that he has re-paid him twice over the amount he kept. And when he could least afford it, too. And his spending what he calls our money without my consent? Why it's his own money; he earns it; he just gives it to me to keep; he has every right to spend it if he likes'.

What about immorality? 'Paul thought a while. "It's very difficult. You see I don't like to hurt Essie's feelings. But she's so unreasonable and absurd. She keeps raving about she'd never believe I was unfaithful to her, even if the evidence was strong against me.'

Martha asked Paul point blank if he had been unfaithful to Eslanda. 'But Paul refused to commit himself. "If I were to admit I am, or had been, what good would it do? She'd never believe it." "Then why worry her?" asked Martha practically. "Well, it puts me in such a false position with myself, to have her insist that I'm true and faithful, when I might not be. I wouldn't mind if she wasn't so sure", he went on in exasperation. "You've no idea how awful it is to go about having her convinced that I'm a little tin god when I'm really far from that.' This, of course, was as good as an admission of guilt.

Eslanda, however, was prepared to forgive. '"Well, darling", she said, looking at him tenderly, "if I ever thought there were lapses, I thought of the possible reasons for them, and dismissed them as not lapses at all. But what I am thoroughly convinced of is this: that no matter what you may have done in these eight years, there has been no change whatever in your love for me except, perhaps, that it has increased. I know that you are faithful to me in the all-important spirit of things; that I am the one woman in your life, in your thoughts, in your love. No matter what other women may have been to you, and you to them, they have in no way walked in my garden. We have kept that sacred to us. I'm not a fool. I love you so much, and understand you so well, and have been so close to you all these years, that I should have known, I should have felt, if you were in any way slipping from me. If there have been others, they have, strangely enough, brought us closer together". Paul's eyes were full of tears, and full of an immense relief.' Eslanda was a truly exceptional woman!

Now it was Eslanda's turn to assert herself. '"Now, if you really wanted to trot out your faults, you should have mentioned your great original sin." "Which is?" "Laziness, with a capital L", she replied emphatically. "It's the cause of most of your shortcomings.'

Eslanda warmed to her task. 'Take your disloyalty to your friends, which is so hard for me to excuse. It's really laziness. When you're away from them, and you usually are, you're actually too lazy to send them a card or write them a letter, though you know how much pleasure it would give them to hear from you. And would you seriously go out of your way to prove to them that you love them? Not you, you're too lazy.'

Eslanda now broached the subject of Paul's music, as she prepared to give him another scolding. '"Take your work. You never learn the lines of your plays until the last moment, when you simply are ashamed to read them any longer. Just think, perhaps if you learned your lines first, then thought about them during rehearsals, and could give your whole attention to direction and action, you might be able to get so much more out of plays than you do. I'm not saying that you don't do very well", she said hastily, "but you might do even better"'.

Here the words of the song 'Ah Still Suits Me' from the film *Show Boat* (1936), in which Paul played the part of 'Joe', a black dockworker, who is being scolded by 'Queenie', his wife, come to mind. Joe:

> Keep on a-naggin',
> 'n bullyraggin',
> 'n criticizin',
> 'n call me pizen,
> Ah ain't apologizin', no siree!
> No matter what you say,
> Ah still suits me.

Despite her criticisms of Paul, Eslanda had 'a great pride in his ability' and was 'seething with ambition' for her husband. Said he, 'Do you really think I could play *Othello* now, if I worked at it?'. I.e. the character 'Othello' in Shakespeare's eponymous play. To this, Eslanda replied, 'I know you can, silly'. And when Paul agreed, '"Attaboy", shouted Essie enthusiastically, placing a resounding kiss on his cheek'.

'I'll have a go at those German songs too', said Paul. 'Larry is always after me to try some over. I do the arias from "The Magic Flute" [Mozart] now, and "The Two Grenadiers", but not well enough to include them on my programmes.' '"That's because you haven't really studied them and thought about them, and worked over them seriously", said Essie promptly; "you could do them magnificently"'. 'All right, I'll try them', said her husband.

Paul was as good as his word, and not long afterwards he told Eslanda, '"I stopped in at Bumpus's yesterday and got a lot of books I wanted"; his eyes danced mischievously'.

Bumpus bookshop, 350 Oxford Street, London. (The Robesons lived in London from 1928 to 1939, as will be seen.)

'"You'll faint when you get the bill; it's about £8". "Good heavens, what on earth did you buy?" "All of Shakespeare's plays; several critical books on him; a swell pocket edition of *Othello*; that new book on Mussorgsky; that two-volume book on Bach; the book of translations of the Schubert songs; the life of Schubert; a marvellous book on Beethoven - and the Gramophone Company is sending me Beethoven's Concerto in D Major with Kreisler and the Berlin State Opera Orchestra playing the

Cesar Franck Symphony; the Schubert Trio in B Flat Major, and a lot more grand records. Very decent of them, isn't it?"'

Modest P. Mussorgsky (1839-1881): Russian composer.

Johann S. Bach (1685-1750): German composer and musician.

Franz Schubert (1797-1826): Austrian composer.

Ludwig van Beethoven (1770-1827): German composer and pianist.

Friedrich-Max ('Fritz') Kreisler (1875-1962): Austrian born US violinist and composer.

Cesar Franck (1822-1890): Belgian-French Romantic composer and organist.

Eslanda was delighted. Said she, 'Days, weeks, months slipped by with Paul spending long hours shut up with his gramophone: playing the fine records over and over; soaking himself in good music; reading his books; buying new books and devouring them; working with Larry; learning songs. He bought a metronome. "That easy rhythm of Negro music has made me careless of the value of notes", he said. He worked hard with his teachers over the new songs. He read *Othello*, and actually learned his lines more than seven months before he was contracted to report for rehearsal'.

It seems doubtful, therefore, that Paul would ever have achieved such mastery of his voice, and in consequence have sung so expressively and so sublimely in his portrayal of joy and happiness, pain, suffering and sadness, had not 'Essie' taken him in hand in the manner described above. Subsequently, in Vienna, Prague, and Budapest she said, 'everywhere ... critics wrote rhapsodic reviews of Paul's voice, his personality, and the music. Hungarians, Austrians, Czechs, proudly entertained him; American ambassadors attended his concerts, congratulated him, and entertained in his honour'.[4]

1. Robeson, Eslanda Goode, *Paul Robeson: Negro*, p.127.
2. Stevenson, A., and Waite, M., *Concise Oxford English Dictionary*.
3. Ibid.
4. Robeson, Eslanda Goode, *Paul Robeson: Negro*, op. cit., pp.128-144.

CHAPTER 16

London (1928-1939)

Said Eslanda in her biography of her husband entitled, *Paul Robeson: Negro*, 'One bright day' in April 1928 'six months after the birth of his [i.e. our] son Paul junior, Paul came home beaming. "Come on, pack your things; we're going to London." "You're joking", said Essie, hoping he wasn't. "Don't you believe it. I'm going to sing 'Ol' Man River' in the London production of *Show Boat*. It's all settled." Essie gaily packed their things'. '*Show Boat* was such a success and had such a long run in London, that the Robesons settled there', she said.[1]

Show Boat: a musical by US composer, Jerome Kern (1885-1945) and US lyricist and theatre producer, Oscar Hammerstein (1895-1960).

At first, said Eslanda, the producers 'did not want to engage Paul for the role of "Joe" in Show Boat'. Paul, they said, was 'too big a man for such a small part'. However, they were 'finally persuaded to engage him, and were surprised and delighted when he built "Ol' Man River" (which Jerome Kern had dedicated to him) into the theme song of the play'.[2]

The outcome was, that on 5 July 1928, British critic, newspaper editor and author, James Douglas, in the UK's *Daily Express* newspaper under the heading, 'A Negro Genius in London' declared, 'I went into the Drury Lane Theatre to hear Paul Robeson singing Negro Spirituals'. The audience 'sat there in a trance of noiseless ecstasy as he touched our heart strings with his marvellous voice. He is more than a great actor and a great singer. He is a great man, who creates the soul of a people in bondage and shows you its true kinship with the fettered soul of man. We became like little children as we surrendered to his magical genius'.

'His songs are the *Bible* as we heard it at our mother's knee', Douglas continued. 'They are the mother-songs of mankind; those hidden songs that all men and women hear in their buried memory. It is not only the dreaming Negro soul that yearns in these cumulative refrains; it is the sad soul of humanity reaching out into the mystery of life and death. I have heard all the great singers of all time. No voice has ever moved me so profoundly with so many passions of thought and emotion. The marvel is that there is no monotony in the spiritual spell. It is effortless enchantment, moving through fluctuant states of thought and feeling.'[3]

Eslanda concluded her biography of her husband by saying of Paul, 'He has friends everywhere. He leaves a trail of friendliness wherever he goes, this Paul Robeson, Negro, who, with his typically Negro qualities - his appearance, his voice, his genial smile, his laziness, his child-like simplicity - is carving his place as a citizen of the world; a place which would most certainly have made his slave father proud'.[4]

Some might regard Eslanda's biography as an exaggeration of her husband's qualities: a eulogy, composed by an adoring wife who saw Paul through the proverbial rose-coloured spectacles. However, numerous film clips exist of Paul in which he comes across *exactly* as she portrays him: a warm and dignified person of great humanity, and also with a genial sense of humour, and yet a man of great intellect and with deep and unwavering principles.

During his time in London, and generally in the numerous other engagements that he fulfilled, Paul demonstrated an extraordinary energy and versatility, despite the fact that Eslanda repeatedly said that he was lazy! And it was in London that he met some of the leading left wingers of the day, including H. G. Wells and George Bernard Shaw.

In April 1928, Paul gave a recital with Lawrence Brown at London's Royal Albert Hall and 'sang spirituals at Sunday afternoon concerts' at the Drury Lane theatre.

In 1929, Paul toured the British provinces and Central Europe. However, 'despite invitations by top London society', he encountered racial discrimination and was refused admission to London's hotels.[5]

On 29 May 1930, Shakespeare's play, *Othello* opened at London's Savoy Theatre with Paul in the role of 'The Moor'. On the opening night there were no less than 'twenty curtain calls'![6] 'When I saw him in Othello', said Lloyd L. Brown, 'the audience was absolutely transfixed'. In the play, said Paul, 'Shakespeare posed this problem, of a black man in a white society'.[7]

In June 1930 in Berlin, Paul appeared as 'Brutus Jones' in a performance of *The Emperor Jones*, a 1920 play by US dramatist, Eugene O'Neill. The play was an oblique criticism of the US occupation of Haiti on 28 July 1915, following bloody rebellions there.

In that year the following events occurred: Paul appeared in the film, *Borderline* (made in Switzerland) with his wife Eslanda; the first biography of Paul entitled, *Paul Robeson: Negro* by Eslanda was published in New York by *Harper & Brothers*; a bust of Paul was sculpted by US/British sculptor, Jacob Epstein (1880-1959); Paul appeared in the UK's *Who's Who* (source of biographical data on influential people throughout the world).[8]

On 29 January 1931, Paul's aunt, Margaret Andrews (née Congleton) died at Cross Roads Township, Martin County.

In the spring of 1931, Paul commenced an affair with British actress, Yolanda Jackson. This lasted for 'about a year and a half', said Paul junior.[9] Meanwhile, Paul and Eslanda separated. The affair was broken off in September 1932 and on 29 October, Paul asked his wife if they could halt the divorce proceedings which they had started and try again. This they did, successfully.

In May 1931, Paul appeared as ship worker, 'Yank Smith' in *The Hairy Ape* by Eugene O'Neill at London's Ambassador Theatre. In that same year, Eslanda enrolled at the London School of Economics to study anthropology. She obtained her Master of Science degree in 1937.) In 1932, Paul and Eslanda were reunited.

On 13 March 1933, *All God's Chillun Got Wings* opened at London's Embassy Theatre, with Paul and British star of stage and screen, Flora Robson.

In May 1933, Paul returned to New York to star in the movie, *The Emperor Jones*. In August he returned to England and began a study of languages in London. Here, he met African students, including Kwame Nkrumah (who became first President of Ghana 1960-1966) and Jomo Kenyatta (who became first President of Kenya 1963-1978).

In August 1933, Paul played a benefit performance of *All God's Chillun Got Wings*: a 1924 play by Eugene O'Neill, in aid of Jewish refugees who had fled Nazi Germany.[10] This was at the urging of Marie Seton (1910-1985), actress, art, theatre, and film critic, and biographer.

When Paul observed 'streams of Jews' arriving in London from Germany, having fled the Nazis, said Harry Belafonte, 'he saw a connection between Nazism for Jews and Nazism for Blacks. There was all this talk about a free world, but there was not even a semblance of freedom for black people around the world at that time'.[11]

Harry Belafonte: Jamaican-US singer, songwriter, and activist.

In September 1933, Paul addressed the Cambridge University Socialist Club.

Paul studied Chinese and Arabic, and he enrolled at the London School of Oriental Languages where he commenced a study of 'West and East Coast African languages'.[12]

In December 1934, Paul was invited to the Soviet Union to discuss with Soviet film director, Sergei Eisenstein (1898-1948) the making of a film about the successful insurrection by self-liberated slaves against

63

French colonial rule in Saint-Domingue, which became the sovereign state of Haiti.

Soviet Union: (official title of the Union of Soviet Socialist Republics, or 'Soviet Union'), existed from 1922 to 1991.

But the film was never produced. In Germany, when en route to the Soviet Union, he was threatened by Nazi storm troopers.[13]

In Moscow, Paul was 'deeply impressed' by the fact that all schoolchildren in the Soviet Union were 'educated against racism'.[14] 'The first time that I stepped on Soviet soil', he said, 'I felt myself a full human being. So it's unthinkable to me, a full human being today, that coloured people in any part of the world would ever join a war or an attack against the Soviet Union'.[15]

Paul saw the Soviet Union, said Tony Benn, as 'an experiment in socialism' which if universally adopted would 'transform the prospects of oppressed people all over the world'.[16]

Tony Benn: Anthony Neil Wedgwood Benn, British politician, writer, and diarist.

'What gripped him', said US historian, David Levening Lewis, was the Russian Constitution, Article 1/23' of which proclaimed 'the complete equality of all citizens in the Soviet Union, and made racism an offence'.[17] Paul resolved to visit that country on an annual basis.

Having returned to London, Paul began a 'study of writings on Marxism and the socialist system in the Soviet Union'.[18]

In May 1935, Paul played the role of 'Bosambo' in a film version of Edgar Wallace's *Sanders of the River*. Paul's expectation was that the film would portray African life and culture in a positive way. He was, therefore, 'enraged' when he discovered that scenes praising British imperialism had been added to the film, without his knowledge. In other words, Paul was being exploited.

Paul now extended his repertoire 'beyond Negro Spirituals, to include Mexican, Scottish, and Russian songs'.[19] As for Paul junior, his favourite song as a child, was 'Shortnin' Bread':[20]

> 'Mommmy's little baby loves short'nin',
> short'nin'
> Mommmy's little baby loves short'nin' bread'

In May 1935, Paul appeared in *Stevedore*, by George Sklar and Paul Peter: a play about the conflict between African American dockworkers and a white racist mob. On 25 September he sailed for the USA in order to make a film of *Show Boat* (1936).[21]

On 15 and 16 March 1936, Paul played the part of Toussaint Louverture in *The Story of the Only Successful Slave Revolt* by Trinidadian historian, journalist, and socialist, C. L. R. James (1901-1989). The play was staged in London's Westminster Theatre.

On 17 August 1936 the British film, *Song of Freedom* was released 'and received praise even from the previously critical American Negro press'. In the film, Paul played 'Johnny Zinga', a black British dockworker who becomes a famous singer, and learns that he is the rightful king of the African island of Casanga.

In September 1936, Paul appeared in the film, *King Solomon's Mines*, based on the book by H. Rider Haggard.

In December and January, Paul visited Soviet Asia and the Caucasus. On 31 December 1936 it was reported from Moscow in the *New York Times*, that Paul would 'place his 9-year-old son in school there "instead of America so the boy need not contend with discrimination because of color until he is older, and his father can be with him"'.[22]

In January 1937, Paul starred in *Big Fella*, a film based on Claude McKay's novel, *Banjo*. Eslanda also played a small part. Unfortunately, said US film journalist, Clyde Taylor, Paul 'never got the chance to play anybody close to what he was, which was a lawyer, a great athlete' and 'a great speaker' with 'a magnificent voice, the voice of the century'.[23]

In February 1937, Paul played 'Corporal Jericho Jackson' in the film *Jericho*, which was filmed in Egypt. This was his first visit to Africa and at last, he had been cast as a heroic and dignified figure. Said Paul junior, 'Paul was the pathfinder, he was finding new directions, he was establishing a different persona for the African American on the screen'.[24]

On 24 June 1937, Paul sang and spoke at London's Albert Hall at a benefit concert for Basque refugees who had fled the Spanish Civil War (17 July 1936 - 1 April 1939). Declaring his support for Republican Spain, he declared that 'the artist must elect to fight for freedom or slavery. I have made my choice. I had no alternative'. In August/September he sang 'at numerous concerts for the Spanish Republican cause'. In October, he polled first place as the singer 'most popular with British radio listeners'. Finally, he announced his intention to retire 'from commercial entertainment'.[25]

In that year of 1937, Paul became co-founder (with African American activist and missionary, Max Jergan) and chairman of the Council on African Affairs, 'formed to aid national liberation struggles in Africa'.

In June 1938, Paul appeared in *Plant in the Sun*, a play by US writer, Ben Bengal (1907-1993) dealing with strikes and union organizing in the USA. It was produced by the Unity Theatre, Cambridge, UK under the auspices of the British Labour Party. In that same month he sang for the International Peace Campaign.

In November 1938, having refused 'roles from major film companies', Paul announced that he would play in *Proud Valley*, a film to be produced by Ealing Studios about an African American who joins a mining community in Wales.

In the winter of 1938, Paul and Eslanda arrived in Spain, where a civil war was raging (17 July 1936 to 1 April 1939). Paul visited the Front and sang to the soldiers of the International Brigade.

International Brigade: military units created by the Communist Internationale to assist the Popular Front government of the Second Spanish Republic during the Spanish Civil War. The Brigade fought on the Republican side against the Nationalist forces of fascist, General Francisco Franco.

Paul also visited hospitals occupied by wounded soldiers and many wounded civilians. It was ironic that here he was, an African American, inspiring Spaniards to fight for their freedom when full freedom was denied to him and his people back at home in the USA.

Said Paul, 'I went to Spain in 1938, and that was a major turning point in my life. There, I saw that it was the working men and women of Spain who were heroically giving their "last full measure of devotion" [a quote from Abraham Lincoln's 'Gettysburg Address' of 19 November 1863] to the cause of democracy in that bloody conflict, and that it was the upper class - the landed gentry, the bankers and industrialists – who had unleashed the fascist beast against their own people'.

'From the ranks of the workers of other lands, volunteers had come to help in the epic defense of Madrid, and in Spain I sang with my whole heart and soul for these gallant fighters of the International Brigade. A new, warm feeling for my homeland grew within me as I met the men of the Abraham Lincoln Battalion - the thousands of brave young Americans who had crossed the sea to fight and die that another "government of the people, by the people, and for the people shall not perish on the Earth". This was another quote from Lincoln's Gettysburg Address'.

'My heart was filled with imagination and love for these white Americans, and there was a sense of great pride in my own people, when I saw that there were Negroes too, in the ranks of the Lincoln men in Spain. Some of them, like African American communist and labour organizer, Oliver Law and African American loyalist [i.e. who supported Spain's democratically elected government], Milton Herndon, were to be among the heavy casualties suffered by the volunteers, and would be buried with their white comrades in the Spanish earth ... a long way from home.'[26]

This was an allusion to one of Paul's favourite Negro Spirituals, 'Sometimes I feel Like a Motherless Child':

> 'Sometimes I feel like a Motherless Child
> 'Sometimes I feel like a Motherless Child
> And Sometimes I feel like a Motherless Child
> A long ways from home.'

On 7 December 1938, Paul sang at the Pavilion Theatre, Cynon Valley, Mountain Ash, South Wales. This was at a meeting to commemorate the 33 Welshmen of the International Brigade who had given their lives in defence of democracy in Spain.[27]

Said Paul, 'The miners of Wales, who gave great support to the anti-fascist movement, welcomed me when I came to sing on behalf of aid to Spain and invited me into their union halls [places of assembly for mining trade unionists] and into their homes. The Welsh miners, and other workers whom I met throughout England and Scotland, made it clear that there was a closer bond between us than the general struggle to preserve democracy from its fascist foes. At the heart of that conflict, they pointed out, was a class division, and although I was famous and wealthy, the fact was that I came from a working-class people like themselves and therefore, they said, my place was with them in the ranks of Labor'.[28]

In January 1939, Paul sang 'at a mass meeting at the Empress Hall in London to greet survivors of two British battalions that had fought for Republican Spain. In April 1939, however, Franco's forces were victorious. On 3 June, Paul and his family returned to the USA.[29]

1. Robeson, Eslanda Goode, *Paul Robeson: Negro,* p.121.
2. Ibid, p.121.
3. Ibid, pp.122-3.
4. Ibid, p.146
5. Foner, Philip S., *Paul Robeson Speaks*, p.29.
6. Ibid, p.29.
7. *'Paul Robeson: Here I Stand', PBS American Masters, 1999.

8. Foner, Philip S., *Paul Robeson Speaks*, op. cit., p.30.
9. *'Paul Robeson: Here I Stand', PBS American Masters, 1999.
10. F p.30.
11. *'Paul Robeson: Here I Stand', PBS American Masters, 1999.
12. Foner, Philip S., *Paul Robeson Speaks*, op. cit., p.30.
13. Ibid, p.30.
14. Ibid, pp.29-31.
15. *'Paul Robeson: Here I Stand', PBS American Masters, 1999.
16. Ibid.
17. Ibid.
18. Foner, Philip S., *Paul Robeson Speaks*, op. cit., pp.29-31.
19. Ibid, p.30.
20. *'Paul Robeson: Here I Stand', PBS American Masters, 1999.
21. Foner, Philip S., *Paul Robeson Speaks*, op. cit., p.31.
22. Ibid, p.31.
23. *'Paul Robeson: Here I Stand', PBS American Masters, 1999.
24. Ibid.
25. Foner, Philip S., *Paul Robeson Speaks*, op. cit., p.31.
26. Robeson, Paul, with Lloyd L. Brown, *Here I Stand*, p.53.
27. Foner, Philip S., *Paul Robeson Speaks*, op. cit., p.32.
28. Robeson, Paul, with Lloyd L. Brown, *Here I Stand*, op. cit., p.54
29. Foner, Philip S., *Paul Robeson Speaks*, op. cit., p.32.

CHAPTER 17

Eslanda's Visit to Africa (1936)

In 1936, Paul's wife Eslanda, now aged 40, broke off from her sojourn in London to pay a prolonged visit to Africa. And she recorded her experiences in her book, *African Journey* (published 1946). As for Paul, he 'couldn't go to Africa with me', Eslanda explained. 'He had contracts ahead for two years to fulfil and couldn't risk not being able to fulfil them.'[1] However, 'our beloved only child', accompanied her on her journey,[2] and on 29 May 1936, 'Pauli [Paul junior] and I took the boat train from London to Southampton for the steamship, *Winchester Castle* of the Union Castle Line'.[3] Destination? Cape Town!

Eslanda began her book with the words:
'I WANTED TO GO to Africa. It began when I was quite small. Africa was the place we Negroes came from originally. Lots of Americans, when they could afford it, went back to see their "old country". I remember wanting very much to see my "old country" and wondering what it would be like.'[4]

Eslanda proved herself a keen and intelligent observer, and *African Journey* is not so much a diary or a travelogue, but a scholarly dissertation. Countries that she visited included not only the Union of South Africa, but also Uganda and the Belgian Congo.

After a few days spent at Cape Town they voyaged onward, and on 18 June 1936 arrived in Port Elizabeth, Cape Province and disembarked. From here, they would commence their journey northward, across country, where Eslanda came face to face with the system of apartheid – a system of segregation on the grounds of race. She described how, at Ntselemantzi, the 'Native location' on the outskirts of the city of Alice, which was situated 140 miles north-east of Port Elizabeth, they visited a native kraal [traditional African village]. 'We went into some of the huts: no windows, no light at all; rough camp beds, cots, pallets on the floor. No sanitation, no water. The lucky ones have a candle or an oil lamp'.

Furthermore, 'the Africans who live here must have permission from the government to do so. Every male of 18 years or over living in this location, must pay the government $5.00 a year poll tax; $3.75 a year hut tax; $3.00 a year ground rent; $1.25 a year dog tax; and $0.25 per head per month, cattle dipping tax'.

'To meet all these taxes and to feed and clothe his family and educate his children (no education is free for Africans in South Africa), the man must, of course, find work. The average and usual work he can find is as herdboy at 25 cents a week, and domestic service at 50 cents a week. Or, he can go to work in the mines at 15 dollars per month. But this he hates to do because it means he must be away from his family from nine to eleven months, doing dangerous and backbreaking work.'

'Out of these magnificent wages', said Eslanda sarcastically, 'he must pay the expenses of transportation to and from the mines, and the inevitable pass fees. These expenses and fees often eat up 15 to 20 per cent of his total wages'.[5]

Pass Laws: a body of laws in operation in South Africa under apartheid, controlling the rights of black people to residence and travel and implemented by means of identity documents compulsorily carried.[6]

Eslanda was not unmindful also, of the plight of a section of the Boer community.

Boer: a member of the Dutch and Huguenot population which settled in southern Africa in the late 17th century.[7]

Said she, 'It is said they are lazy, shiftless, and ignorant, but these accusations are familiar to us. The same things are said about Negroes, to ease the consciences of those who grind us down. The same economic exploitation accounts for the desperate plight of Negroes and poor Whites.'[8]

Poor Whites: members of an impoverished white underclass.[9]

Finally, for the African, said Eslanda, there was no recreation. 'They have only their work in domestic service, on the farms, or on the railway beds [i.e. laying railway tracks]'.[10]

Eslanda soaked up all the information she could about the black peoples of Africa: information that would be conveyed to her husband, and put to good use in his unending campaign on their behalf.

In respect of education, said Eslanda, 'Christians were the first modern educators in Africa. Now African education rests upon the church. Probably, 85 per cent of all education in Africa is carried on by the missionary and Christian African personnel; in many places with Government subsidies but in many others, without any'.[11] She concluded, 'If the present state of affairs continues, in which only about 10 per cent of native children get any education, whatever (and perhaps 2 or 3 per cent any education worthy of the name), we shall naturally not arrive at that general background of changed ideas from which alone a new social tradition can spring.'[12]

Eslanda concluded by saying, in bold letters, 'Africans are people'.

1. Robeson, Eslanda Goode, *African Journey*, p.13.
2. Ibid, p.14.
3. Ibid, p.17.
4. Ibid, p.9.
5. Robeson, Eslanda Goode, *African Journey*, op. cit., pp.46-7.
6. Stevenson, A., and Waite, M., *Concise Oxford English Dictionary*.
7. Ibid.
8. Robeson, Eslanda Goode, *African Journey*, op. cit., p.52
9. Stevenson, A., and Waite, M., *Concise Oxford English Dictionary*, op. cit.
10. Robeson, Eslanda Goode, *African Journey*, op. cit., p.54.
11. Ibid, p.100.
12. Ibid, p.173.
13. Ibid, pp.186-7.

CHAPTER 18

Paul's Attitude to Colonialism

Film footage exists of Paul being interviewed on television in Australia in 1960 by Australian novelist and journalist, Ronald McKie and Australian concert pianist and television presenter, Eunice Gardiner.

Looking immaculate in dark suit, white shirt, and tie, Paul gestured expressively with his hands as he made his points. Sometimes he was serious, with furrowed brow; but every so often, his face lit up in a broad smile. He was neither belligerent nor aggressive, but charming as always. However, the interviewers were left in no doubt as to who was in control of the interview. For here was a mighty man, in every sense of the word: physically, intellectually, morally.

Bearing in mind, said McKie, that the American Negro 'had for so long been an American second-class citizen'. "And still is, I'm sorry!", Paul interrupted. Nevertheless, continued Mackay, the Negro 'had contributed so much to culture, for example, in music and dance'. Paul agreed. Said he, both 'The Africans and the American Negroes have turned out to be an extraordinarily gifted people. The great tragedy is, that by not making us first-class citizens, as yet, in America they may be losing, I don't know how much' i.e. talent.

Did Paul regard himself as an American, or as an African? 'I would say that, unquestionably, I am an American. Born there, my father a slave there. Upon the backs of my people was developed the primary wealth of America.'

'Just like the Scottish American is proud of being from Scotland', said Paul, 'I'm proud of being an African. In our schoolbooks they tried to tell me that all Africans were savages'. But when he arrived in London, said Paul, he 'found that most of the Africans I knew were going to Oxford and Cambridge'.

Someone, presumably British, said Paul, had had 'the temerity' to suggest to him that Negroes were a 'backward people'. And yet, this person's forebears had 'imposed upon the Chinese people the opium trade'. So, 'this didn't make any sense at all' when the Negro 'had been civilised for so long'.

'It was wonderful', said Paul, 'to find that the coloured peoples of the world were very advanced. So, I would say today that I'm an American', but one 'who is infinitely prouder' for being 'of African descent. No question about it. I'm an Afro-American, and I don't use the word "American" ever loosely again'.

Why did Paul decide to return to the USA, having lived in London for more than a decade (from 1928 to 1939)? Said he, 'I felt I had to go back to my people, because the going [for them] was tough'. And times were still tough now. 'I could get a telegram, next week', he said, telling him that 'a new group of people had gathered in one of the "Congresses", and say, "Paul, with the difficulties that are going on in America, would you come back and help us?" If so, he 'would take the plane as soon as I finish my engagements'.

Congresses: derivatives of the National Negro

Congress, founded in 1936 with the goal of advancing the social, political, and economic prospects of African Americans.

Eunice asked, 'Were the Negro people of the USA organized, gathered together, all of a piece?' 'We are very religious people', Paul replied. 'My father was a part of the church school, the AME Zion Church, which was founded in 1796. My brother is pastor of one of the largest churches in New York, the mother church. It led the struggle for freedom in the time of slavery.'

There were no less than 18 million, or so, Negro Christian worshippers in the USA, said Paul. 'We are the most organized people on the face of the Earth. We are so organized, that if the Negro people of New York, Michigan, Illinois, and the main populated states of America tomorrow, this week, decide to vote as one unit, if they ask, is Nixon going to help the negro people most? Do we think he will? Or Kennedy? Whichever way we decide, *we* will decide who is president of the United States. That's how organized we are. We are of one mind on this. We want our freedom. We want to be full citizens, not second class.'[1]

Richard Milhous Nixon: 37th President of the US, serving from 1969 until 1974.

John Fitzgerald Kennedy ('JFK'): 35th President of the US from January 1961 until his assassination in November 1963.

---

1. 'Paul Robeson on Colonialism: African American Rights', Spotlight, ABC Education, 1960.

CHAPTER 19

Return to the USA (1939)

On 3 June 1939, the Robesons returned to the USA, where Paul appeared 'in a short run' of a revival of *The Emperor Jones*. On 1 July he gave his first song recital, following his return, at Mother AME Zion Church in Harlem, where his brother, the Reverend Benjamin Robeson was pastor.[1]

In August 1939, Paul refused to appear in the musical drama, *John Henry* (based on the life of the eponymous African American folk hero) in Washington DC 'because the theatre was segregated. It opened in New York instead'.[2]

On 1 September 1939 the Second World War commenced.

In October 1939, was subjected to a further indignity when he arrived for tea having been invited by a 'leading New York City hotel' and was 'told to use freight elevator'.[3]

On 5 November 1939, 'Ballad for Americans', an operatic cantata with lyrics by US lyricist and musician, John La Touche and music by US composer, arranger and folk music singer-songwriter, Earl Robinson, was sung by Paul and broadcast to the nation by the CBS (Columbia Broadcasting System, NYC). Its first verse contains a reference to the year 1776 and the US Declaration of Independence on 4 July.

Paul instantly became a national hero, and the CBS received more telephone calls praising that broadcast than had been the case for any programme previously aired.

The year 1940 was a rollercoaster of ups and downs. In January Paul was 'criticized by some newspapers for refusal to participate in a fund-raising affair for Finns in Russo-Finnish War'. In July he was 'refused service in a fashionable San Francisco restaurant'. Whereupon he sued the owner 'for $22,500 under California Civil Code barring discrimination in public places on basis of race or color'.[4]

On 23 July 1940, Paul sang 'Ballad for Americans' 'to 30,000 people jamming Hollywood Bowl', a modern amphitheatre in the Hollywood area of Los Angeles. In September, he appeared 'with pianist, Hazel Scott and novelist, Richard Wright at a benefit [concert] for the 'Negro Playwrights Company' before 5,000 people at the Golden Gate Ballroom in Harlem'.[5]

In May 1941, Paul spoke at a rally in downtown Detroit in aid of the UAW (Unite Auto Worker's Union).[6]

On 7 December 1941, the USA entered the Second World War. Paul supported the war effort, said Belafonte, by encouraging people to buy war bonds and liberty bonds (issued by the government to finance wartime expenditure), 'pointing out to black people that we had a responsibility to be part of that struggle, even if we had to make alliances with people who were traditionally our enemy'.[7]

Throughout 1942, Paul performed at rallies, recorded programmes, and gave recitals, 'many at no fee', in aid of US and Allied soldiers.[8] On 8 April, Paul addressed 'a mass meeting in New York City's Manhattan Center called to "mobilise Negro and colonial people in the fight against fascism"'.[9] In May, he addressed 51,000 workers at Yankee Stadium (baseball park, NYC) and called for the opening of a 'second front to shorten the war'.[10]

On 10 August 1942, Paul appeared in his first US performance as 'Othello', in the eponymous play by William Shakespeare. The play opened at the Brattle Hall in Cambridge Massachusetts, under the direction of US-British theatre actress and producer, Margaret Webster. In that same month, Paul appeared in his last commercial film, *Tales of Manhattan*.[11]

On 19 October 1943, Paul appeared in *Othello*, with German-US actress and theatre practitioner, Uta Hagen as 'Desdemona', in a Theatre Guild production, which opened on Broadway's Schubert Theatre 'to tremendous critical and audience acclaim'.[12] But for Paul, this marked the beginning of an affair with the show's leading lady. Said Uta, 'We had a three-year relationship which started rather early in the run [of *Othello*] in New York'.[13] On 30 June 1944, *Othello* closed in New York 'after a record run of 296 performances'.[14]

On 7 May 1945, the war in Europe officially ended. During that year, Paul continued to work tirelessly in support of workers and their trade unions. Said US trade union leader, Henry Foner, Paul 'always emphasised this need for unity between the black people and the unions. Neither could advance without the other'.[15]

On 2 September 1945, the war against Japan officially ended.

In September 1946, Paul joined in sponsoring the 'Crusade against Lynching', representing a coalition of some 50 organizations. As a delegate to Washington, he asked Harry F. Truman, 33rd (Democratic)

President of the United States to issue "formal public statement" that would make clear his [the President's] views on lynching'.[16]

Between 1882 and 1935, a total of 1,288 Whites and 3,380 Blacks were known to have been lynched in the USA. Between 1936 and 1948 the corresponding figures were 1 White and 54 Blacks.[17] These figures should be viewed in the context that Blacks represented only about 10% of the US population in those times.

In October 1946, Paul was elected vice-president of the Civil Rights Congress, a US civil rights organization founded in 1946.[18]

In that year of 1946, Eslanda obtained her PhD degree in anthropology from Hartford Seminary, Hartford, Connecticut.

In March 1947, Paul sang 'I Dreamed I Saw Joe Hill' (lyrics by Alfred Hayes, British-born screenwriter and poet, and music by Earl Robinson), at the University of Utah, Salt Lake City. This was a song very close to Paul's heart.

> 'I dreamed I saw Joe Hill last night
> Alive as you and me
> Says I, "But Joe, you're ten years dead"
> "I never died" says he
> "I never died" says he
> "The copper bosses killed you, Joe"
> "They shot you Joe", says I
> "Takes more than guns to kill a man"
> Says Joe "I didn't die"

Joe Hill (born Joel Emmanuel Hägglund) was a Swedish-American trade union activist, employed at the Silver King silver and copper mine, Park City, Utah. Hill was charged with the murder of John G. Morrison and his son, Arling at nearby Salt Lake City Utah. Found guilty, he was executed by firing squad on 19 November 1915.[19] A subsequent investigation indicated that his conviction was very likely to have been a miscarriage of justice.

Afterwards, Paul made the following announcement: 'You have just heard my final concert for at least two years, and perhaps for many more. I'm retiring here and now from concert work. I shall sing now for my trade union and college friends. In other words, only at gatherings where I can sing what I please'.[20]

On 9 May 1947, the Board of Education of Albany, New York, denied permission for a Paul Robeson concert at Philip Livingston Junior High School. This was on the grounds that neither the board, nor the city, 'will subsidise, commission, or have anything to do with Communism'.[21] The decision was overturned by the Supreme Court, and the concert went ahead.[22]

In June 1947, Paul gave four concerts in Panama in support of Panamanian workers who were attempting to form trade unions.[23] On 29 June, at Winston-Salem, NC, Paul spoke in support of the 'Local 22', the Food, Tobacco, Agricultural, and Allied Works Union of America.[24] In March 1948, Paul toured the Hawaiian Islands on behalf of the International Longshoremen's and Warehousemen's Union, accompanied by Lawrence Brown and Earl Robinson'.[25]

In that year of 1948, Paul sought 'an appointment with President Truman' in order to 'confer' with him 'on anti-poll tax, anti-lynching, and fair employment legislation'. However, his 'repeated requests' were rejected.[26]

In June 1948, Paul appeared before the US Senate committee which was holding hearings on the 'Mundt-Nixon Bill'. Formerly known as 'The Subversive Activities Control Act', the Bill was named after US Republican Congressmen, Karl E. Mundt and Richard M. Nixon. Drafted by the House Un-American Activities Committee (HUAC), this called for the registering of Communist Party members and 'Communist Front' organizations. Paul opposed the measure on the grounds that it violated the rights of US American citizens. When asked if he would fight in a war with the Soviet Union, Paul replied, 'That would depend on conditions'. When asked if he was a member of the Communist Party, he refused to answer the question.[27] This was not the last that Paul would hear of the HUAC.

In July 1948, Paul pledged his strong support for the Progressive Party, a new political party founded the previous year. In a speech, he poured scorn on the two main parties, Democratic and Republican, which were contesting the forthcoming election: 'What mockery! Our high standard of living for a minority in the richest country of the earth! Absentee ownership still ruled supreme. One per cent of the population owns as much wealth as one-third of the ill-housed, ill-fed, whom Roosevelt so feelingly described'. And he spoke of 'the contempt of big business barons for the great majority of the American people'.[28]

In January 1949, Paul addressed a protest meeting called by the newly organized 'Negro Youth Builders Institute'. Said he, 'the suppression of the Negro in the United States varies only in degree in New York, New Jersey, Georgia, and Alabama'. He remarked on 'children in cotton fields in the South', and 'children on tobacco plantations and exploited children all over', and on the 'neglected children of the North'. The 'pattern' was the same, he said: 'evidence of a coloured minority in a hostile white world'.[29] And all this, 8 decades after so-called 'Emancipation'!

In February 1949 Paul commenced a concert tour of the UK. On 25 March 1949, at Friend's House, the central office of the Quakers in London, he led a protest against the apartheid politics of the South African government. It was attended by about 3,000 people.[30]

1. Foner, Philip S., *Paul Robeson Speaks*, p.32.
2. Ibid, p.32.
3. Ibid, p.32.
4. Ibid, p.32.
5. Ibid, p.33.
6. Ibid, p.33.
7. *'Paul Robeson: Here I Stand', PBS American Masters, 1999.
8. Foner, Philip S., *Paul Robeson Speaks*, op. cit., p.33.
9. Ibid, p.33.
10. Ibid, p.33.
11. Ibid, p.33.
12. Ibid, p.33.
13. *'Paul Robeson: Here I Stand', PBS American Masters, 1999.
14. Foner, Philip S., *Paul Robeson Speaks*, op. cit., p.34.
15. *'Paul Robeson: Here I Stand', PBS American Masters, 1999.
16. Foner, Philip S., *Paul Robeson Speaks*, op. cit., p.35.
17. Archives at Tuskegee Institute.
18. Foner, Philip S., *Paul Robeson Speaks*, op. cit., p.35.
19. National Coal Board (NCB) Film.
20. Foner, Philip S., *Paul Robeson Speaks*, op. cit., p.35.
21. Duberman, Martin Bauml, *Paul Robeson*, p.319.
22. Foner, Philip S., *Paul Robeson Speaks*, op. cit., p.36.
23. Ibid, p.36.
24. Ibid, p.36.
25. Ibid, p.36.
26. Ibid, p.36
27. Ibid, p.36.
28. Ibid, pp.36-7.
29. Ibid, p.37.
30. Ibid, p.37.

CHAPTER 20

The Paris Peace Conference (20-24 April 1949): Jackie Robinson

At the 'Soviet Union-sponsored' World Congress of Partisans for Peace (Paris Peace Conference) 20-24 April 1949, Paul sang the famous ballad, 'Joe Hill'. This was 'just as the Cold War was beginning to intensify'.

The event was described by US writer, Gilbert King in the *Smithsonian Magazine* 13 September 2100. Paul 'addressed the audience and began speaking extemporaneously, as he often did, about the lives of black people in the United States. We in America, do not forget that it is on the backs of the poor Whites of Europe ... and on the backs of millions of black people that the wealth of America has been acquired. And we are resolved that it shall be distributed in an equitable manner among all of our children, and we don't want any hysterical stupidity about our participating in a war against anybody, no matter whom. We are determined to fight for peace. We do not wish to fight the Soviet Union'.[1]

However, in an anonymous article the *Associated Press* (US news agency, headquarters NYC) distorted Paul's words as follows: 'It is unthinkable that American Negroes would go to war, on behalf of those who have oppressed us for generations, against the Soviet Union, which in one generation has lifted our people to full human dignity'.

'By the next day', said King, 'the press was reporting that Robeson was a traitor.'

Meanwhile, unbeknown to Paul, Roy Wilkins and Walter White of the National Association for the Advancement of Colored People (NAACP) 'were pressured by the U.S. State Department to issue a formal response to the singer's purported comments. The NAACP, always wary of being linked in any way to communists, dissociated itself from Robeson. Channing Tobias, a member of the NAACP board of directors, called him "an ingrate"'.[2]

Ingrate: an ungrateful person.[3]

In July 1949, Jack 'Jackie' Roosevelt Robinson, US professional baseball player and the first African American to play in Major League Baseball in the modern era, was summoned to Washington DC by John

Wood, a Georgia Democrat, and current chairman of the HUAC. To the HUAC, Robinson stated as follows:

'The fact that it is a communist who denounces injustice in the courts, police brutality, and lynching when it happens, doesn't change the truth of his [Paul's] charges. Just because communists kick up a big fuss over racial discrimination when it suits their purposes, a lot of people try to pretend that the whole issue is the creation of communist imagination.' In other words, Robinson's message was, 'Don't shoot the messenger!'

Had Robinson any comment to make about Paul's statement made in Paris 'to the effect that American Negroes would refuse to fight in any war against Russia because we love Russia so much'? Robinson replied as follows: 'If Mr Robeson actually made it [the alleged statement], it sounds very silly to me. But he has a right to his personal views ...'.

In fact, Paul was quite open in his views. He said subsequently, 'I'm an anti-fascist and I would feel, perhaps, that any war against the Soviet Union would be a fascist war. Why not talk about peace and friendship with the Soviet Union?'[4]

Finally, as far as the fight against racial discrimination was concerned, said Robinson, 'We can win our fight without the communists and we don't want their help'.[5]

Continued King, 'Everyone, from conservatives to Eleanor Roosevelt, criticized the singer.

Eleanor Roosevelt, widow of President Franklin D. Roosevelt and former US First Lady from 1933-1945 during her husband's four terms in office.

'The former First Lady and civil rights activist noted, "Mr. Robeson does his people great harm in trying to line them up on the Communist side of political picture. Jackie Robinson helps them greatly by his forthright statements".'

As a result, 'the backlash against Robeson was immediate. His blacklisting and the revocation of his passport rendered him unable to work or travel, and he saw his yearly income drop from more than $150,000 to less than $3,000. In August 1949 he managed to book a concert in Peekskill, New York, but anti-civil rights factions within the American Legion, and Veterans of Foreign Wars caused a riot, injuring hundreds, thirteen of them seriously'.

'Robeson's name was stricken from the college All-America football teams.'

College Football All-America Team: an honour given annually to the best American college football players at their respective positions.

'Newsreel footage of him was destroyed, recordings were erased and there was a clear effort in the media to avoid any mention of his name.'[6]

Almost seven years later Paul himself, would be brought before HUAC and asked to identify members of the Communist Party and to admit to his own membership of it.

'Towards the end of his life, Jackie Robinson had a chance to reflect on the incident and his invitation to testify before HUAC. In his autobiography, entitled *I Never Had It Made*, he wrote, "I would reject such an invitation if offered now. I have grown wiser and closer to the painful truths about America's destructiveness. And I do have increased respect for Paul Robeson who, over the span of twenty years, sacrificed himself, his career and the wealth and comfort he once enjoyed because, I believe, he was sincerely trying to help his people".'[7]

On 25 February 1948, in a coup d'etat, the Communist Party of Czechoslovakia, with Soviet backing, had gained control of the democratic government of President Edvard Beneš of the ČSNS party. (Beneš resigned on 7 June 1948.)

ČSNS party: Czech National Social Party, founded 1897.

At the Cultural and Scientific Conference for World Peace (Waldorf Conference), held at the Waldorf Astoria Hotel, NYC, 25-27 March 1949 and sponsored by the National Council of American-Soviet friendship, Paul spoke in favour of peaceful relationships with the Soviet Union.[8] His speech was soon to have unfortunate repercussions for him.

In spring 1949, Paul arrived in Czechoslovakia with his wife, Eslanda to sing in the Prague Spring International Music Festival (14 May – 6 June). The invitation had been issued by the Czech government.

1. King, Gilbert, 'What Paul Robeson Said', *SMITHSONIANMAG.COM*, 13 September 2011.
2. Ibid.
3. Stevenson, A., and Waite, M., *Concise Oxford English Dictionary*.
4. *'Paul Robeson: Here I Stand', PBS American Masters, 1999.
5. Testimony of Jackie Robinson before the HUAC, 18 July 1949, FBI via the Digital Library of Georgia.
6. King, Gilbert, 'What Paul Robeson Said', op. cit.
7. Robinson, Jackie, *I Never Had It Made*, p.86.
8. Foner, Philip S., *Paul Robeson Speaks*, p.39.

CHAPTER 21

Further Strivings (1949-1953)

On Tuesday 13 May 1949, Paul visited Woolmet Colliery near Edinburgh, Scotland, where he sang, unaccompanied, to the awestruck miners. The song he chose was 'I Dreamed I saw Joe Hill'.[1]

Also, in May 1949, Paul visited Poland's Warsaw ghetto, and was deeply moved. Created by the Nazis on 12 October 1940, all Jewish residents of Poland's capital had been ordered to relocate to this designated area. Here, they were deliberately starved, died from disease, or were removed to Treblinka and other extermination camps. The total death toll in the ghetto was estimated to be in the region of 400,000.

On 4 June 1949, Paul arrived in Moscow where the 150th anniversary of the birth of Russian poet, Alexander Pushkin was being celebrated. Paul asked to see his friend, Soviet Yiddish poet, Itzik Feffer, but Feffer was being held in Moscow's notorious Lubyanka Prison. Nevertheless, he was brought to Paul's hotel. Feffer guessed that the hotel was bugged, so they communicated by way of written notes.

Shortly afterwards, at a concert in the Tchaikovsky Concert Hall, Moscow, which was broadcast live, nationally, Paul made a point of describing how he had recently seen Feffer. And he concluded by singing, in Yiddish, the 'Hymn of the Partisans' of the Warsaw Ghetto: 'Zog Nit Keynmol'.[2]

Yiddish: a language used by Jews in, or from, central and eastern Europe.[3]

> 'Never say that you're going your last way,
> Although the skies filled with lead cover blue
>   days.
> Our promised hour will soon come;
> Our marching steps ring out: "We are here!".'

Three years later, on 12 August 1952, Feffer was executed, as part of Soviet Premier, Josef Stalin's plan to eliminate the major intellectual and artistic figures of the Jewish community.[4]

Joseph Vissarionovich Stalin: a Georgian revolutionary and Soviet politician who ruled the Soviet Union from the mid-1920s until his death in 1953.

On 14-16 June 1949, 'Two Worlds', a three-part series, was published in *Komsomolskaia Pravda*, the Journal of Communist Youth in the USSR (Soviet Union). In an article by Paul entitled, 'First Joy' he recalled impressions of his first visits to that country in 1934 and 1936.[5]

On 16 June 1949, Paul returned to New York having completed a four-month tour of Europe and the Soviet Union. On his return, he was asked by reporters if it was true that there was a purge in the Soviet Union. Paul denied it. In other words, he could not bring himself to criticise the country that he admired so much and preferred to remain 'in denial'.

Paul now described the trial of 11 Communist leaders, which was currently taking place, as 'a type of domestic fascism'. He also 'denounced Wall Street's 'War Policy'.[6] The leaders were accused of violating the Smith Act, a statue that prohibited advocating the violent overthrow of the government.

On 19 June 1949, Paul junior, currently a student at Cornell University, Ithaca, NYC was married to Marilyn Paula Greenberg, a white student who was also studying at Cornell.

On 27 June 1949, *Time* magazine published an interview in which Paul declared his confidence that, from the Soviet experience (i.e. the Russian Revolution of 1917), Africans would free themselves in the near future. He also emphasised 'that the Negro people must come to identify themselves with the workers' – i.e. the working class.[7]

On 29 June 1949, Paul spoke at a protest rally in Madison Square Garden held by the Civil Rights Congress.

On 27 August 1949, the 'Peekskill Riots' began, at a concert that took place at Corlandt Manor, Peekskill, Westchester County, New York State. These were race riots directed against African Americans and Jews, in the course of which Paul was prevented from singing. Undeterred, he announced, 'I'm going to sing wherever the people want me to sing. My people and I won't be frightened by crosses burning in Peekskill, or anywhere else'.

On the night of the concert, 6 crosses were burned at Tallahassee, Florida, more than 1,000 miles away, each with a sign on it saying, 'We protest Paul Robeson and Communism'. And at Peekskill, one cross was burned on a nearby hillside. Cross burning is a practice associated with the Ku Klux Klan.

On 4 September 1949, a second concert was held at Peekskill: this time, successfully. However, mob violence ensued with injuries to about 140 people. Meanwhile, state troopers did nothing to prevent the attacks, and in some instances encouraged mob rule.[8]

On 9 September 1949, Eslanda visited Mexico City to address about 1,000 delegates at the Continental Congress for Peace.[9]

On 13 March 1950, Paul was barred by the National Broadcasting Company (NBC: US commercial radio and television network) from appearing on Eleanor Roosevelt's television programme, scheduled for 19 March. An NBC spokesman stated that 'no good purpose would be served in having him speak on the issue of Negro politics'.[10]

On 28 June 1950, Paul spoke out against US participation in the Korean War.

On 28 July 1950, Paul refused to surrender his passport as agents of the State Department had ordered. On 1 August, Paul's lawyers asked the State Department for an explanation of the order. On 7 August, the Chief of Passport Division replied that 'the action was taken because the Department considers that Paul Robeson's travel abroad, at this time, would be contrary to the best interests of the United States'.[11]

On 28 August 1950, the State Department offered to restore Paul's passport 'if he will sign a statement that he will not make any speeches while abroad'. He refused.[12]

In 1951, at the 'American People's Congress of Peace', held from 29 June - 1 July in Chicago, Paul, in an address to an audience of about 7,000, again criticised US action in Korea.[13]

On 5 November 1951 in NYC, Paul addressed the opening session of the 'Conference for Equal Rights for Negroes in the Arts', Sciences, and Professions.[14]

On 15 November 1951, Paul, together with Soviet Ambassador to the USA, Alexander S. Panyushkin and US socialist philosopher, Corliss Lamont, addressed the 'World Peace Rally', sponsored by the National Council of American-Soviet Friendship in NYC.

On 17 December 1951, Paul headed the New York delegation presenting a petition to the UN by the Civil Rights Congress, declaring genocide against Negroes of US on the grounds that '15 million black Americans are mostly subjected to conditions making for premature death, poverty, and disease'.[15]

On 31 January 1952, Paul attempted to cross the US border to Canada where he had been invited to address a meeting of the Mine, Mill, and

Smelter Workers Union in Vancouver, BC. However, he was advised by a State Department representative that if he left the USA, he would be subject to five years' imprisonment and a fine of $10,000. He therefore, spoke and sang to the meeting by telephone from Seattle, Washington State, USA.[16]

In April 1952, Paul wrote 'My Pop's influence is still present in the struggles of today. I know he would say, "Stand firm, son; stand by your principles". To which Paul added, "You bet I will, Pop – as long as there is a breath in my body"'.[17] Hence the title of Paul's autobiography, *Here I Stand*.

In the early 1950s the Othello Recording Corporation was founded as an independent label in NYC, to enable Paul to record his music. In December 1952, the corporation issued the album 'Robeson Sings' which included 'Wandering', 'Four Rivers', 'Witness', 'My Curly-Headed Baby', 'Night' (in both Russian and English), and 'Hassidic Chant'. However, recording companies refused to issue his records or to record new ones, and he found all concert halls and theatres closed to him.[18]

1. National Coal Board (NCB) Film.
2. *'Paul Robeson: Here I Stand', PBS American Masters, 1999.
3. Stevenson, A., and Waite, M., *Concise Oxford English Dictionary*.
4. *'Paul Robeson: Here I Stand', PBS American Masters, 1999.
5. Foner, Philip S., *Paul Robeson Speaks*, p.37.
6. Ibid, p.38.
7. Ibid, p.38.
8. Ibid, p.38.
9. Ibid, p.38.
10. Ibid, p.39.
11. Ibid, p.39.
12. Ibid, p.39.
13. Ibid, p.40.
14. Ibid, p.40.
15. Ibid, p.40.
16. Ibid, p.40.
17. Robeson, Paul, 'Here's My Story', *Freedom*, Volume II, Number 4, April 1952, p.5.
18. Foner, Philip S., *Paul Robeson Speaks*, op. cit., p.41.

CHAPTER 22

Eslanda Testifies to the HUAC (7 July 1953)

Paul's wife, Eslanda was summoned to appear before the elaborately named Senate Permanent Sub-committee on Investigations of the Committee on Government Operations in Washington DC, and she gave her testimony on 7 July 1953. Chairman of the committee was the notorious, Senator Joseph R. McCarthy.

Joseph Raymond McCarthy (1908-1957) was US Republican senator for Wisconsin from 1942 until his death in 1957. It was as a result of the activities of this rabble rouser (not to say 'witch hunter') –in-chief, that the term 'McCarthyism' entered the language. This was the practice of making accusations of subversion or treason without proper regard for evidence. McCarthyism was prominent in the USA during the period of the 'Red Scare' (late 1940s and 1950s).

In the Western World, sensitivities were heightened in regard to communism by the fact that on 1 October 1949, Chinese Communist leader, Mao Zedong had announced the creation of the People's Republic of China.

Roy M. Cohn, Chief Council to the HUAC began by asking Eslanda if she was the author of a book entitled, *African Journey*? And was she also the author of a biography of her husband? The answer to both questions was yes.

Cohn: Now, Mrs Robeson, are you a member of the Communist Party?

Eslanda: Under the protection afforded to me by the 5th and 15th Amendments, I decline to answer.

Whereupon Chairman McCarthy pointed out that 'The 15th Amendment has nothing to do with it. That provides the right to vote'. He continued, 'Negro or white, Protestant or Jew, we are all American citizens here, and you will answer the question as such. The question is: Are you a Communist today? If you feel the answer will tend to incriminate you, you can refuse to answer'.

McCarthy had adopted the hectoring, bullying, even menacing tone for which he was notorious. But this gave Eslanda the opportunity for which she had been waiting.

Eslanda: 'What confuses me a little about what you said - you see I am a second-class citizen in this country and, therefore, feel the need of the 15th. That is the reason I use it. I am not quite equal to the rest of the white people'.

McCarthy persisted. 'The question is: Do you feel if you tell us the truth, a truthful answer would tend to incriminate you?' Eslanda did not fall into the trap!

Eslanda: 'I would not consider any answer except the truth. I would certainly not be bothered with any untruthful answer'.

McCarthy repeated the question, saying, 'We are going to make you answer that'. Said she, 'I do not understand the truthful part. Certainly, the answer would be truthful. Under any circumstances whatsoever it would be truthful. That is the reason you are confusing me'.

Stuart Symington, Democratic Senator for Missouri, now 'took over as acting chairman', and Cohn resumed his questioning.

Cohn: 'Mrs Robeson, have you ever contributed royalties from your writings to the Communist Party?' Eslanda made no reply.

G. David Schine, Chief Consultant to the HUAC now asked Eslanda, 'Mrs Robeson, did you write this book all by yourself?'

Eslanda: 'All by myself'.

Schine: 'This *African Journey*?'

Eslanda: 'Well, I don't quite understand that question'. One could almost feel Eslanda's hackles rising!

Schine: 'Did you receive help on this book?'

Eslanda: 'Well, I really think that is a very insulting question. I am quite capable of writing a book. I did write this book all by myself'.

Cohn: 'Have you ever engaged in sabotage or espionage, Mrs Robeson?'

Eslanda: 'I don't know what sabotage and espionage are'.

Cohn: 'Have you have ever engaged in any illegal act against the United States?'

Eslanda: 'Not to my knowledge'.

Cohn: 'Have you ever taught or advocated the Communist Party?'

Eslanda: 'I have never taught anywhere at any time'.

Cohn: 'Do you believe in the overthrow of the government of the United States by force and violence under any circumstances?'

Eslanda: 'Under no circumstances whatsoever'.

Cohn: 'Have you ever heard that the overthrow of this government of the United States was taught or advocated at any Communist Party meeting?'

Eslanda: 'Well, I have never heard it advocated at all anywhere and I don't believe it'.

Eslanda was then asked repeatedly by Symington whether she had ever been a member of the Communist Party. Finally, failing to receive a reply he asked her. 'Do you think you are a good American?'

Eslanda: 'I know I am'.

Symington: 'You couldn't be a good American and at the same time dedicated to the overthrow of the government by force and violence'.

Eslanda: 'I don't know anything at all about the Communist Party except what I read in the papers or hearsay, and I would not dream of making a statement here from what I read in books'.

Symington made one last attempt. Had Eslanda ever been, or was she now a member of the Communist Party? She refused to answer.[1]

During her interrogation, Eslanda had blazed a brilliant trail, answering only those questions which she chose, and using the experience as a platform to argue for the rights of 'the Negro'. Three years later her husband, Paul would also be summoned by the HUAC and acquit himself equally well.

In early August 1953, Paul applied for a passport to travel to England, France, Norway, Sweden, and Denmark. His request was denied by the Passport Office.[2] Two years later, on 16 August 1955 Federal Judge Bunita S. Matthews refused to order the State Department to restore Paul's passport. However, the implication was that the passport could be issued if he agreed to sign a non-Communist oath. Paul refused.[3]

---

1. U.S. Senate, Senate Permanent Subcommittee on Investigations of the Committee on Government Operations, Washington DC, 7 July 1953.
2. Foner, Philip S., *Paul Robeson Speaks*, p.41.
3. Ibid, p.41.

CHAPTER 23

Paul Testifies to the HUAC (12 June 1956)

On 7 June 1956, Paul's wife Eslanda, had testified before the Senate Permanent Sub-committee on Investigations of the Committee on Government Operations, and she had acquitted herself admirably. Now, three years later, on 12 June 1956, Paul himself testified before the House Un-American Activities Committee (HUAC), having been subpoenaed (ordered by writ to attend) by the committee to do so.

If members of the HUAC thought that they were going to intimidate Paul and pummel him into submission, how wrong they were! For what they did, inadvertently, was to offer him a platform from which to broadcast his message countrywide, if not worldwide, and thus afford him maximum publicity for his efforts!

The HUAC was an investigative committee of the US House of Representatives. It was created in 1938 to investigate alleged disloyalty and subversive activities on the part of private citizens, public employees, and organizations suspected of having fascist or communist ties. (The Committee was abolished in 1975.) During the HUAC's 37-year existence, hundreds of people were hauled up before it.

The truth is, that those who were hauled up to appear before the HUAC included some of the most talented and creative people in the USA. For example: actor and film maker, Charlie Chaplin; actor, director, writer, and producer, Orson Welles; musician and folklorist, Alan Lomax; lyricist and librettist, 'Yip' Harburg; and of course, Paul Robeson himself.

Chairman of the HUAC (from January 1955 to 1963) was Democrat and member of the US House of Representatives for Pennsylvania, Francis E. Walter.

The atmosphere at the HUAC meeting was toxic from the beginning. Paul was asked to swear 'to tell the truth, the whole truth, and nothing but the truth', by an official, in a sneering and contemptuous voice. This set the tone for the entire proceedings. But if anyone thought that he would be intimidated, they would find themselves sadly mistaken. Paul had demonstrated his courage on many occasions: for example, on the football field. He would now demonstrate it again, before the HUAC.

Richard Arens was Counsel for the HUAC - and former aide to Senator McCarthy which says it all! Paul was asked by Arens whether, when he had applied for a passport in July 1954, he had been asked to sign an affidavit stating that he was not a Communist. To this, Paul replied that, 'under no conditions would I think of signing any such affidavit, that it is a complete contradiction of the rights of American citizens'. He was then asked if he was 'now a member of the Communist Party?' He refused to answer the question, saying, 'I invoke the 5th Amendment'.

5th Amendment to the US Constitution: No person 'shall be compelled in any criminal case to be a witness against himself'.

What Paul did say, however, was this: 'Gentlemen ..., wherever I have been in the world, Scandinavia, England, and many places, the first to die in the struggle against Fascism were the Communists and I laid many wreaths upon graves of Communists'.

Arens: 'Have you ever been known under the name of "John Thomas"?'

Robeson: 'My name is Paul Robeson'.

Paul's lawyer, Milton Friedman now asked if the photographers present might now take their pictures. This prompted a sarcastic response from Paul! As far as being photographed was concerned, he said, 'I am used to it and I have been in moving pictures. Do you want me to pose for it, good? Do you want me to smile? I cannot smile when I am talking to him [a reference to Arens]'.

Did Paul know a person name Nathan Gregory Silvermaster? Silvermaster, of Russian-Jewish descent, had served as an economist with the US War Production Board during the Second World War. He was also a spy for the Soviets but was never formally charged. Again, Paul refused to answer, invoking the 5th Amendment no less than four times.

HUAC member, Gordon H. Scherer, lawyer, and US Congressman for Ohio (1933-1941) said of Paul, 'The witness talks very loud when he makes a speech, but when he invokes the 5th Amendment, I cannot hear him'. Paul replied, 'I invoked the 5th Amendment very loudly. You know I am an actor, and I have medals for diction. Oh, gentlemen, I thought I was here about some passports', and he described the proceedings as 'complete nonsense'.

Walter admitted that it was, 'by a unanimous vote, that this Committee has been instructed to perform this very distasteful task'. 'To whom am I talking?' Paul enquired. This was a huge and calculated 'put down' by Paul, because compared to himself, Walter was a virtual nonentity! 'You are speaking to the Chairman of this Committee', he said.

Robeson: Mr. Walter?
Walter: 'Yes'.
Robeson: 'The Pennsylvania Walter?'
Walter: 'That is right'.
Robeson: 'Representative of the steelworkers?'
Walter: 'That is right'.
Robeson: 'Of the coal-mining workers and not United States Steel, by any chance? A great patriot'. Paul supported anyone who represented the working class.
Walter: 'That is right'.

However, now came a passage in the proceedings, during the course of which Walter, with the eyes of the world upon him (via the radio and television), would reveal his innermost, hateful, and despicable prejudices.

Robeson: 'You are the author of all of the bills that are going to keep all kinds of decent people out of the country'.
Walter: 'No, only your kind'.
Robeson: 'Colored people like myself, from the West Indies and all kinds. And [it is] just the Teutonic Anglo-Saxon stock that you would let come in'.
Walter: 'We are trying to make it easier to get rid of your kind, too'.
Robeson: 'You do not want any colored people to come in?'

This was an extraordinary admission by the chairman of the HUAC himself. Walter wished to rid the USA of all black people, despite the fact that they had been brought to the country (as slaves and against their will since at least the mid-1520s).

For example, in 1526, a Spanish expedition to establish an outpost on the North American coast in present day South Carolina, included a contingent of enslaved black Africans. Therefore, tens of thousands of such slaves had lived in the USA for far longer than millions of other, more recent, white immigrants. This was racial prejudice of the most blatant and insidious kind!

Robeson was finally permitted to voice his feelings, a decision which the committee was subsequently to regret! He made it clear that in his opinion, the charge against him of being a communist was a smokescreen, and what the authorities really hated was the way he sought equality for the black community with the white, not only in the USA but further afield. The real reason why he was debarred from travelling abroad was, he said, 'because I have struggled for years for the independence of the colonial peoples of Africa. For many years I have so labored and I can say modestly that my name is very much honored all over Africa in my struggles for their independence. That is the kind of independence like Sukarno got in Indonesia'.

Sukarno (1901-1970): Indonesian politician who had led the Indonesian struggle for independence from the Dutch Empire. This independence was officially recognised on 2 November 1949, in an agreement signed by the Dutch.

The other reason, said Paul, was 'that when I am abroad, I speak out against the injustices against the Negro people of this land. I sent a message to the Bandung Conference and so forth'.

Bandung Conference (18-24 April 1955): the first large-scale Afro-Asian conference – a meeting of Asian and African heads of state, most of which were newly independent.

'That is why I am here. This is the basis, and I am not being tried for whether I am a Communist; I am being tried for fighting for the rights of my people, who are still second-class citizens in this United States of America.'

'My mother was born in your state, Mr. Walter, and my mother was a Quaker, and my ancestors in the time of Washington, baked bread for George Washington's troops when they crossed the Delaware, and my own father was a slave.'

'I stand here struggling for the rights of my people to be full citizens in this country. And they are not. They are not in Mississippi. And they are not in Montgomery, Alabama. And they are not in Washington. They are nowhere, and that is why I am here today. You want to shut up every Negro who has the courage to stand up and fight for the rights of his people, for the rights of workers, and I have been on many a picket line for the steelworkers too. And that is why I am here today.'

When Paul was asked by Arens if he had visited Europe and the Soviet Union in 1949, he said yes. He described the Soviet people as 'one of the finest musical audiences in the world', and he spoke of the great Soviet composers and great musicians, 'very cultured people, and Tolstoy, and ...' Here, the chairman interrupted saying, 'We know all of that', but by now Paul was warming to his task! Said he, 'They have helped our culture and we can learn a lot'.

When Paul was in Paris, said Arens, did he 'tell an audience there that the American Negro would never go to war against the Soviet government?' This was a reference to the Paris Peace Conference, 20-24 April 1949.

Paul referred Arens to a speech that he had made in London, which was attended by '2,000 students from various parts of the colonial world: students who since then have become very important in their governments, in places like Indonesia and India, and in many parts of Africa'. These students, said Paul, represented 'populations that would range to 6 or 7 hundred million people'.

The students, Paul continued, 'asked me and Mr. Dadoo, a leader of the Indian people in South Africa ... to say there that they were struggling for peace, that they did not want war against anybody'.

Yusuf M. Dadoo (1909-1983): South African communist and anti-apartheid activist.

Bernard William Kearney, a Republican Congressman, lawyer, army officer, and HUAC member asked Paul, 'Do you know anybody who wants war?' Referring to his Paris speech, Paul declared, 'No part of my speech ... says 15 million American Negroes would do anything. I said it was my feeling that the American people would struggle [i.e. strive] for peace, and that has since been underscored by the President of these United States'. Not for nothing had Paul learned and honed his debating skills whilst an undergraduate at Rutgers University!

Kearney repeated the question, but Paul ploughed on undeterred. 'Listen to me. I said it was unthinkable to me that any people would take up arms, in the name of an Eastland, to go against anybody.'

James O. Eastland: a former Democratic Senator who had opposed racial integration and described Blacks as 'an inferior race'.[1]

'Gentlemen, I still say that. This United States Government should go down to Mississippi and protect my people. That is what should happen.'

Arens then showed Paul an article attributed to him from the *Daily Worker*, dated 3 July 1949, entitled 'I Am Looking for Full Freedom'.

The *Daily Worker*: a newspaper published in NYC by the Communist Party USA.

'At the Paris Conference', said Paul, 'I said it was unthinkable that the Negro people of America or elsewhere in the world could be drawn into war with the Soviet Union'. Furthermore, in his opinion, it was 'quite clear that no Americans, no people in the world probably, are going to war with the Soviet Union. So, I was rather prophetic, was I not?'

Arens now quoted from a speech that Paul had made when he was in Sweden.

Robeson: 'Let me listen'.
Arens: 'Do so, please'.
Robeson: 'I am a lawyer'.
Kearney: 'It would be a revelation if you would listen to counsel'.
Robeson: 'In good company, I usually listen'.

The inference was obvious. Paul regarded the present company as far from good!

Arens: 'I do not hesitate one second to state clearly and unmistakably: I belong to the American resistance movement which fights against American imperialism, just as the resistance movement fought against Hitler'.

Paul did not deny that this was what he had said, and he added, 'Just like Frederick Douglass and Harriet Tubman were underground railroaders, and fighting for our freedom, you bet your life'.

Frederick Douglas: the son of a white master and a black slave, he wrote his autobiography and with $600 earned in royalties, he purchased his freedom.

Arens continued to read aloud from Paul's alleged Sweden speech.

Arens: 'If the American warmongers fancy that they could win America's millions of Negroes for a war against those countries, then they ought to understand that this will never be the case. Why should the Negroes ever fight against the only nations of the world where racial discrimination is prohibited, and where the people can live freely? Never! I can assure you they will never fight against either the Soviet Union or the peoples' democracies'.

Had Paul made that statement? 'I do not remember that', he replied. Nonetheless, he admitted that it was broadly true. Whereupon, Kearney declared, 'The witness has answered the question and he does not have to make a speech ...' But by now, Paul was not to be stopped! When he was in Russia, he said, 'I felt for the first time like a full human being. No color prejudice like in Mississippi; no color prejudice like in Washington. It was the first time I felt like a human being. Where I did not feel the pressure of color as I feel in this Committee today'.

Scherer asked Paul why he had not remained in Russia? This provided the opportunity for another major salvo on Paul's part! Said he vehemently, 'Because my father was a slave, and my people died to build this country, and I am going to stay here, and have a part of it just like you. And no fascist-minded people will drive me from it. Is that clear? I am for peace with the Soviet Union, and I am for peace with China, and I am not for peace or friendship with the fascist Franco, and I am not for peace with fascist Nazi Germans. I am for peace with decent people'.

Scherer: 'You are here because you are promoting the Communist cause'.

Robeson: 'I am here because I am opposing the neo-fascist cause which I see arising in these committees'. Paul was now well and truly on the proverbial warpath!

When Walter told Paul that there was 'no prejudice' i.e. against African Americans, this led to a further instant rebuke.

Robeson: 'Just a moment. This is something that I challenge very deeply, and very sincerely: that the success of a few Negroes, including myself or Jackie Robinson, can make up for [a paltry income of] 700 hundred dollars a year for thousands of Negro families in the South'. Paul pointed to a study of the subject by Columbia University. 'My father was a slave, and I have cousins who are sharecroppers, and I do not see my success in terms of myself.' In other words, he was part of a far wider movement.

Sharecropper: a tenant farmer who gives a part of each crop as rent.[2]

'That is the reason my own success has not meant what it should mean: I have sacrificed literally hundreds of thousands, if not millions, of dollars for what I believe in.'

Had Paul praised Stalin when he was in the Soviet Union, asked Arens? Whereupon Paul stated that he was not prepared to discuss Stalin 'with a representative of the people who, in building America, wasted 60 to 100 million lives of my people, black people drawn from Africa on the plantations. You are responsible, and your forebears, for 60 million to 100 million black people dying in the slave ships and on the plantations'.

On the subject of slavery, said Arens, 'While you were in Soviet Russia, did you ask them there to show you the slave labor camps?' As far as he knew, said Paul, those camps housed 'fascist prisoners [i.e. Nazis] who had murdered millions of the Jewish people, and who would have wiped out millions of the Negro people, could they have gotten a hold of them'.

Arens could have made more of this. For example, he could have drawn Paul's attention to the existence of the 'gulags', written about from personal experience by Solzhenitsyn and others, where political dissidents were held in frightful conditions.

Aleksandr Solzhenitsyn (1918-2008): Russian novelist, historian, and political prisoner and an outspoken critic of communism.

Or of the fact that in the Soviet Union, police informers lurked on every corner: in the factories; in blocks of flats; in the communes (communal settlements in communist countries[3]). And Paul himself was naïve, in not realising that the Soviets had shown him only what they wanted him to see, and that this land of so-called freedom and equality, was in fact, a dictatorship; a gigantic police state, where human rights were virtually ignored, opposition to the government was not tolerated, and there was no freedom of speech.

Arens: 'Now I would invite your attention, if you please, to the *Daily Worker* of 29 June 1949, with reference to a get-together with you and Ben Davis. Do you know Ben Davis?'

Benjamin Jefferson Davis junior (1903-1964): African American lawyer and communist.

This gave Paul yet another opportunity to air his views, to the exasperation of Chairman Walter!

Davis, said Paul, was 'One of my dearest friends, one of the finest Americans you can imagine, born of a fine family, who went to Amherst and was a great man'.

Amherst College: liberal arts college in Amherst, Massachusetts.

Walter: 'The answer is yes?'

Once again, Walter, and Arens likewise, were playing straight into Paul's hands!

Robeson: 'Nothing could make me prouder than to know him'.

Walter: 'That answers the question'.

Arens: 'Did I understand you to laud his patriotism?'

Robeson must have thought Christmas had come early!

Robeson: 'I say that he is as patriotic an American as there can be, and you gentlemen belong with the Alien and Sedition Acts, and you are the non-patriots, and you are the un-Americans, and you ought to be ashamed of yourselves'.

Walter, who realised that he and his committee had lost the unequal struggle, against Paul, the world figure, the superb debater, with the forensic mind of the trained lawyer, was now at the end of his tether.

Walter: Just a minute, the hearing is now adjourned.

'I should think it would be', Paul declared.

'I have endured all of this that I can', said Walter, who had by now well and truly 'lost it'!.

Robeson: Can I read my statement?

Walter: No, you cannot read it. The meeting is adjourned.

Robeson: 'I think it should be, and you should adjourn this forever, that is what I would say'.[4]

Game, set, and match to Paul! Not for nothing had Paul won the oratorial contest at Rutgers three years in a row! In his clinical dismantling of the HUAC and its case against him, he had acted with great composure, whilst not compromising his principles in the slightest. His opponents, meanwhile, had 'lost their rag' and had finished in total disarray. Paul had 'fought the good fight' and his father, William Drew – 'Pop' – would have been justly proud of him.

Why did Paul not simply say, no, I am not a member of the Communist Party? Because he considered it to be none of the HUAC's business!

1. Hunter, Marjorie, 'James O. Eastman is Dead at 81: Leading Senate Foe of Integration', *The New York Times*, 20 February 1986.
2. Stevenson, A., and Waite, M., *Concise Oxford English Dictionary*.
3. Ibid.
4. Source: Congress, House, Committee on Un-American Activities, *Investigation of the Unauthorized Use of U.S. Passports*, 84th Congress, Part 3, June 12, 1956; in *Thirty Years of Treason: Excerpts from Hearings Before the House Committee on Un-American Activities, 1938–1968*, Eric Bentley (editor), *Viking Press*, New York, 1971.

CHAPTER 24

1956-1958

In the 1956 edition of *College Football and All-American*, Paul's name was deliberately omitted from the list of players who featured in the Walter Camp's All-American team in 1918.[1]

On 26 May 1957, Paul sang via 'a new coaxial-cable' link 'to an audience of 1,000 in England' at 'a conference sponsored by the National "Let Paul Robeson Sing" Committee'.[2]

On 1 August 1957, Paul sang in a 'comeback concert' to a packed house in the Third Baptist Church in San Francisco'.[3]

On 4 September 1957, the first day of classes at Central High School, Little Rock, Arkansas, Governor Orval Faubus called in the Arkansas National Guard to block the entry of nine black students. Later that month, President Dwight D. Eisenhower sent in federal troops to escort the 'Little Rock Nine' into the school.[4]

On 23 September 1957, Paul demanded that the US government uphold the Constitution and combat racism in the town of Little Rock.[5]

In December 1957, Paul was invited by the miners of Wales to be their honoured guest at that year's Eisteddfod. Once again, the US Supreme Court denied him a passport, but he circumvented the court by singing 'on schedule ... via a trans-Atlantic [telephone] hookup' between New York and the town of Porthcawl on the South Wales coast.[6]

In March 1958, Indira Gandhi, daughter of Indian Prime Minister Nehru, convened a national committee in order 'to sponsor a "Paul Robeson Day" in the Indian capital Delhi, on the occasion of Paul's forthcoming 60th birthday on 9 April.[7]

Jawaharlal Nehru: First Prime Minister of India.

On 9 April 1958, Paul's 60th birthday was celebrated in Berlin in the German Democratic Republic; in Peking, 'and in many African nations'.[8]

On 10 May 1958 Paul gave his first concert for a decade in NYC's packed Carnegie Hall and told the 'cheering audience' that his passport had finally been restored to him.[9]

On 4 August 1958, Paul sang at the Welsh National Eisteddfod in the steelmaking town of Ebbw Vale in South Wales.[10]

On 15 August 1958, Paul commenced a tour of the Soviet Union.[11] He appeared on Moscow television, sang at the Moscow Sports Palace, and met with Soviet Premier, Nikita Khrushchev at Yalta in the Crimea.[12] In that same month of August, Paul's autobiography, *Here I Stand* was published in London by *Dennis Dobson*; in New York by *Othello Associates*; in Bucharest, Romania by *Editura Politica*; in Berlin by *Congress-Verlag*; in Moscow by both *Molodaia Guardiia* and *Pravda*. However, no leading US publisher deigned to publish his book.[13]

On 17 September 1958, Paul commenced a tour of the German Democratic Republic.[14]

In October 1958, Paul was presented with a miner's lamp by the miners of Wales.[15] And in November, Paul sang at a concert in London's St Paul's Cathedral, to an audience of about 4,000 people seated within, and another 5,000 people standing without.[16]

1. Foner, Philip S., *Paul Robeson Speaks*, p.42.
2. Ibid, p.42.
3. Ibid, p.42.
4. *Wikipedia*.
5. Foner, Philip S., *Paul Robeson Speaks*, op. cit., p.42.
6. Ibid, p.42.
7. Ibid, p.42.
8. Ibid, p.42.
9. Ibid, p.42.
10. Ibid, p.42.
11. Ibid, p.42.
12. Ibid, p.43.
13. Ibid, p.43.
14. Ibid, p.43.
15. Ibid, p.43
16. Ibid, p.43.

CHAPTER 25

Wales: A Welcome in the Valleys for Paul (1957 and 1958)

Paul's association with Wales and its people was one of longstanding. In London on 8 November 1927, as he was making his way home after a matinee performance of *Show Boat*, he became aware of singing which came from a group of 270 Welsh miners. They were protesting against the Ministry of Health's refusing, or limiting relief for unemployed miners and their families, and also against the Government's new Unemployment Bill. 'On impulse', said Paul junior, 'he fell in with them'.

The coal owners had responded to the miners' grievances in the following way, said Paul's Welsh friend, Martha Edwards. 'They blacklegged the whole lot of them, and they locked them out of the colliery. Thousands of them, not just a handful'. As for the miners, 'They couldn't just leave the pit and find a job elsewhere. There *was* nothing else. Many, many families were on the verge of starvation. And this group said, "We've got nothing to lose. Let's go all the way to London. They've got plenty up there. We've got nothing. We're like a forgotten race"'.

The miners had, therefore, marched the 165 miles from their homes in Wales's Rhondda Valley to London, in a desperate attempt to find a way to obtain a remedy for their grievances. Without hesitation, Paul joined the 'Hunger March', and on the steps of a building in the city, he gave a rendition of 'Ol' Man River'.

Paul paid for the miners to be provided with food and clothing, and he also gave a donation so that they could return home by train. Said UK journalist, Philip Dewey, 'It was a selfless act of kindness that would be remembered by those miners, and it was the start of a blossoming relationship between Robeson and Wales'.[1] Until Paul met with the miners, said Martha with a broad smile, 'he didn't even know there was a place called Wales'.[2]

On the tour which followed, Paul sang to audiences in Cardiff, Neath, and Aberdare, and visited the Talygarn miners' rest home in Pontyclun.[3]

In the presence of the miners, as film footage reveals, there was a radiant joy on Paul's face. This was no act. He was in his element. The oppressed people of Wales were just as dear to him as the oppressed people of Harlem, or anywhere else for that matter.

Some 50 years later Paul's son, Paul junior visited the Miners' Rehabilitation Centre at Talygarn and met an elderly man who had been present on that day of Paul's visit in 1929.[4]

On 22 September 1934, there was an underground explosion at Gresford Colliery near Wrexham in North Wales. A fire ensued, and 266 men lost their lives. Later that year, Paul performed at Caernarfon, North Wales, in a benefit concert for victims of the disaster. Subsequently, at the Majestic Cinema in Wrexham, Paul gave a charity performance, staged for the benefit of the St John Ambulance Association.

Martha recalled a disaster which had occurred when she was a child, at another Welsh colliery. 'The coal owners – the bosses - arrived in a car, and the first thing they asked was, "Were there any pit ponies killed or injured in the explosion". They never asked about the men. They asked about the pit ponies. They had to buy the pit ponies, of course'.

In 1940, *The Proud Valley*, which was filmed on location in the Rhondda Valley, was released. It tells the story of David Goliath 'a black American man who comes to Wales to find work and strikes up a friendship with the Welsh mining community, as he helps to better their working conditions and ultimately sacrifices his own life to save the lives of his colleagues in a mining disaster'.[5]

Of all his films, said Paul, this was his favourite. 'It's from the miners in Wales I first understood the struggle of Negro and White together', he declared.[6]

By early 1957, Paul's passport had still not been renewed. However, with encouragement from Welsh Labour politician, Aneurin Bevan (credited for his contribution to the founding of the UK's post-Second World War Welfare State) whom he had met during his time in the UK, Paul discovered a way of getting his voice heard. 'He conducted a series of concerts in Wales and London by singing over a transatlantic telephone cable.'[7]

On 5 October 1957, a concert was held at the Grand Pavilion, Porthcawl on the South Wales coast as part of the miners' Eisteddfod, with about 5,000 people in attendance. Via the transatlantic cable Will Painter, the union leader, was able to address Paul directly. Said he, 'We are happy that it has been possible for us to arrange that you speak and sing to us today', but 'We would be far happier if you were with us in person'. To this, Paul replied, his voice booming out over the loudspeakers, 'My warmest greetings to the people of my beloved Wales, and a special hello to the miners of South Wales at your great festival. It is a privilege to be participating in this historic festival'.

Paul performed a selection of his songs and dedicated them to the struggle for what he called 'a world where we can live abundant and dignified lives'. Whereupon, the Treorchy Male Choir (founded in 1883), winners of that year's Eisteddfod and Paul, joined together to sing the Welsh national anthem, 'Land of My Fathers'. Finally, the entire audience serenaded Paul with a rendition of 'We'll Keep a Welcome'. 'This land you knew will still be singing', they chorused, 'When you come home again to Wales'.[8]

In August 1958, Paul visited Wales in person, his passport having been restored to him the previous May. On 4 August, as already mentioned, he sang at the National Eisteddfod, Ebbw Vale, and addressed an adoring audience.

1. Dewey, Philip, 'The Story of Paul Robeson and the Unbreakable Bond he formed with the Miners of Wales', WalesOnline, 14 April 2019
2. *'Paul Robeson: Here I Stand', PBS American Masters, 1999.
3. Sparrow, Jeff, 'How Paul Robeson found his Political Voice in the Welsh Valleys', *The Observer*, Biography Books online, 2 July 2017.
4. Ibid.
5. Dewey, Philip, 'The Story of Paul Robeson and the Unbreakable Bond he formed with the Miners of Wales', op. cit.
6. Ibid.
7. Ibid.
8. Sparrow, Jeff, 'How Paul Robeson found his Political Voice in the Welsh Valleys', op. cit.

CHAPTER 26

1959: Paul Returns to Czechoslovakia (1959)

Paul's passport had been confiscated in July 1950. However, 'it was restored in 1958, following the landmark Kent vs. Dulles case'.

Rockwell Kent (1882-1971): US painter and illustrator who was repeatedly denied a passport on the grounds that he was allegedly a communist.

John Foster Dulles: US Secretary of State.

In the case of Kent versus Dulles, the US Supreme Court stated that the right to travel is part of the 'liberty' of which a citizen cannot be deprived without due process of law under the 5th Amendment.

In 1959, Paul returned to Czechoslovakia, again at the invitation of the Czechoslovak government, this time for the International Congress of Socialist Culture (organized by Czechoslovak communists). It was held at Prague's Industrial Exhibition Ground in June.

Although he stayed for less than two days, Paul was star guest, along with the Soviet composer, Dmitri Shostakovich and he was 'given a rapturous welcome by the 2,000 delegates at Prague's Trade Fair Palace'. When Paul addressed the assembled gathering, he began with the words 'Jak se mate?' ('How are you?') in Czech. It should be remembered that he was fluent in several languages.

Paul continued, 'It is a great privilege and pleasure to be again with you here in Prague, to greet my dear friends, the people of Czechoslovakia, and to greet you, many friends from many lands. My deepest thanks for your concern over many years, for your help and for your encouragement. And this is true not only of myself, but of many of us in America, who have consistently struggled for peace and friendship with you and with all the peoples of the lands of socialism'.

'The speech went on to heap praise on the Soviet Union', said US broadcaster, journalist, and for eight years, Editor in Chief of Radio Prague, David Vaughan.

Paul continued, 'On recent visits to the Soviet Union, it was wonderful to see the development, the new cultural growth of many peoples in the eastern sections, like Uzbekistan, who have leapt across the centuries into the present and into the future. How inspiring to see the wealth of talent among the youth and in the factories. How wonderful to hear today of the rich potential of the people of your great land, of the deep interest of the workers, in all phases of their complex life, of their demands for a rounded reflexion of this life in our creative, cultural activities'.

Said Vaughan, 'But the speech was not just about the achievements of the Soviet Union. The theme of the International Congress was culture, and Robeson put forward his ideas of the role of culture in socialism'.

Said Paul, 'Throughout the ages, the great roots of culture have come from the people, the great genius has come from them'. And on a lighter note, 'I don't need to apologise for my beard – I'm playing "Othello" over in Stratford [-on-Avon] in England and thinking of the great Shakespeare. There, where he walked and lived, I hear the speech of the people of Warwickshire today. The great Shakespeare spoke their language. And the language that he used and uses in his great tragedies and comedies is the result of centuries of creative activity. The very language itself has come from, and was created by the people, wherever they may be. Any language comes from them'.

Paul went on to mention Czech composer, musical theorist, and folklorist, Leoš Janáček (1854-1928), whom he described as 'a great musician, who understood so much of the richness of his people's language that the very melody of his music is the melody of the speech of the peoples of Czechoslovakia'.

As for 'your great' Czech composer, Antonín Dvořák (1841-1904), said Paul, he 'came to our land and heard the beautiful songs of my folk. And he pointed out to us in America that here was the basis of a great musical art, springing from a people who had been torn from Africa and brought in slavery to the lands of America'.

This was a reference to Dvořák's residency in the USA (from 1892 to 1895), where he took up the post of Director of the National Conservatory in NYC. Here, Dvořák was inspired by the music of both African Americans and Native Americans.

Dvořák's 'influence still has great importance in America today', said Paul.

Said journalism student, Lam Nguyen of Paul, 'In his speech, most of the time he speaks English, but then he also speaks Russian, because he expects the others probably to understand him and he also wanted to show his personal attachment to the socialist cause. And it was interesting that he also sang – Russian songs. It definitely brightened up the speech, to make it less boring during that conference! His voice captures the whole hall'.

Paul would have been wiser, however, to have addressed his audience in their native language, Czech: Russian being an alien language that the Czechs were forced to learn at school under the communist regime.

Finally, said Paul, 'We want you to know, that in our part of the world, there are millions who want peace with the lands of socialism. And we will find peace. As one of the songs goes: Peace will conquer war – "Mir pobedit voynu". Thank you – "Děkuju!"'.

These were fine words, but as Paul would discover, in communist Czechoslovakia, things were not always quite what they seemed!

In 1967, Czech-Canadian writer and publisher, Josef Škvorecký's novella, *The Bass Saxophone* was published (by Lester & Orpen, Toronto). Škvorecký (1924-2012) had immigrated to the USA after the Soviet invasion of his country in 1968.

In the preface to *The Bass Saxophone*, Škvorecký presented an entirely different viewpoint, when he articulated what many Czechs had thought about Paul's visit to their country 18 years previously, in 1959. They loved his singing, his songs, and his warm personality, but realised that he was misguided in thinking that the Czechs had freedom in any meaningful sense of the word. Said Škvorecký, 'They pushed Paul Robeson at us. And how we hated that black apostle who sang of his own free will at open-air concerts in Prague, at a time when they were raising the socialist leader, Milada Horáková to the gallows: the only woman ever to be executed for political reasons in Czechoslovakia by Czechs, and at a time when the great Czech poets, some 10 years later to be rehabilitated without exception, were pining away in jails'.

Milada Horáková (born 1901): Czech politician and member of the underground resistance movement during the Second World War. She was tried on a fabricated charge of conspiracy and treason, convicted, tortured, and hanged on 27 June 1950.

In other words, the Czechs realised, even if Paul did not, that the Czech communist rulers saw his visit as a propaganda coup and had used the great singer as a pawn in the Cold War game.

Škvorecký continued, 'Well, maybe it was wrong to hold it against Paul Robeson. No doubt he was acting in good faith, convinced that he was fighting for a good cause. But they kept holding him up to us as an exemplary "progressive jazz man", and we hated him. May God rest his - one hopes - innocent soul'. Škvorecký evidently believed that Paul's motives were honourable, but that he was naïve.

Almost a decade after Paul's visit, on 20-21 August 1968, the Warsaw Pact invaded Czechoslovakia.

Warsaw Pact: the Soviet Union, Poland, Bulgaria, East Germany, and Hungary.

This action, said Vaughan, 'brought an end to any remaining illusions about the Soviet Union's intentions' as far as that country was concerned.[1]

In November 1989, after the non-violent, so-called 'Velvet Revolution', the Communist government of Czechoslovakia was toppled.

On 10 December, a predominantly non-communist government was appointed. This ended 41 years of one party, communist rule. In February 1990, Soviet troops began to withdraw from that country; the withdrawal being completed by 1 July 1991.

1. Vaughan, David, 'Paul Robeson in Czechoslovakia: All Culture Comes from the People', Radio Prague International, 26 August 2017.

CHAPTER 27

1961-1976

In January 1959, on a visit to Moscow, Paul was welcomed by Premier Nikita Khrushchev. But Paul fell ill and was admitted to hospital. He had been a cigarette smoker, which did not help. In January 1960, Paul revisited Moscow and was again greeted by Khrushchev.

On 27 March 1960, when he was again in Moscow, Paul attempted suicide. Said his friend, Helen Rosen, Paul 'cut his wrists and one could see the scars, but he never talked about it'. Said Paul junior, 'They found him early enough so that he didn't bleed severely enough to be in danger'. Eslanda travelled to Moscow to be with him and 'he recovered rapidly under the Soviet doctors' recommended treatment'.[1]

But why? Said Paul junior, 'It's a myth that he was suffering over the years from the classic, cyclic [bipolar] depression'. There was 'no such medical evidence throughout his life' to support this notion. Instead, Paul junior suspected that his father had been drugged by a person unknown, with a drug developed by the CIA as part of a programme called MK-Ultra. The programme was 'designed to make a person paranoid and suicidal'.[2]

Paul's granddaughter, Susan Robeson stated that 'there were levels at which the health issues impacted his capacity. He certainly got depressed'.[3]

In March 1961, Paul again visited Moscow, but his health was poor, and he was again hospitalised for a time.

In mid-September 1961, Paul was admitted to London's Priory (Psychiatric) Hospital, where he was given no less than 54 ECTs. (ECT: electroconvulsive therapy.) This was 'outrageous by any standards then, or now', said Paul junior. Finally, Paul travelled to East Berlin where he was admitted to the Buch Clinic, and his health improved.[4]

In 1963, Eslanda was diagnosed with breast cancer, but even when her condition became terminal, said Paul's biographer, Martin B. Duberman, she decided to keep that news from her husband 'because she wanted Paul to be spared. Essie did a lot of that throughout her life, trying to protect and spare Paul'.[5]

On 1 December 1963, Paul's brother, the Reverend Benjamin C. Robeson died at Bronx, NYC at the age of 70, having been pastor at the Mother AME Zion Church for twenty-seven years.[6]

On 22 December 1963, Paul returned to the USA, after an absence of more than 5 years. Whereupon, he was asked by reporters what he was going to do now. 'I'm going to be resting for a while', he replied. Would he be taking any part in the Civil Rights Movement? 'I've been a part of it all my life', he said.[7]

There is an air of unreality about seeing Paul on film as an elderly man, bespectacled, grey at the temples, anxious, lined, and slower in his movements. 'If I can't be Paul Robeson, I will retire', he told Lloyd L. Brown.[8]

On 27 August 1964, Paul spoke at the funeral of Benjamin J. Davies, 'Communist leader in Harlem and close friend'.[9]

On 25 October 1964, Paul issued a statement praising the German Democratic Republic 'on the 15th anniversary of its founding'.[10]

German Democratic Republic: a country that existed from 1949 to 1990, when the eastern portion of Germany was part of the Eastern Bloc during the Cold War.

In winter 1965, Paul published an article entitled, 'The Legacy of W. E. B. Dubois' in *Freedomways*.[11] On 13 December 1965, Eslanda died, aged 68. She was buried at Ferncliffe Cemetery, Hartsdale, Westchester County, New York.

Freedomways: the leading African-American theoretical, political and cultural journal of the 1960s to the 1980s.

William Edward Burghardt Du Bois (1868-1963): African American sociologist, socialist, historian civil rights activist, Pan-Africanist, author, writer and editor.

In December 1970, the head football coach and president of Rutgers University criticised 'the failure of the National Football Foundation to select Paul Robeson, twice [an] All-American, for its Hall of Fame'.[12]

On 27 December 1971, Lawrence Brown, composer, vocalist 'and famous recreator of Negro Spirituals and folk songs' and Paul's 'accompanist and companion for many years', died in hospital in Harlem.[13]

In 1972, said Lloyd L. Brown, '*Ebony* prints a list: "Ten Greatest Black Men in America"'.

Ebony: a Chicago magazine, specially designed for African Americans.

'Paul looks at this. He thought about it for a while, and then he said, "Pop would have been proud". After all these years, he's still the child, bringing home the [school] report card'.[14]

On 15 April 1973 a 'Salute to Paul Robeson', a cultural celebration of Paul's 75th birthday (an event which had occurred on 9 April) was held at a packed Carnegie Hall, NYC.[15] In that year of 1973, Paul's brother, Reeve died at Sioux City, Woodbury, Iowa.

1. *'Paul Robeson: Here I Stand', PBS American Masters, 1999.
2. Ibid.
3. Ibid.
4. Ibid.
5. Ibid.
6. Foner, Philip S., *Paul Robeson Speaks*, p.44.
7. *'Paul Robeson: Here I Stand', PBS American Masters, 1999.
8. Ibid.
9. Foner, Philip S., *Paul Robeson Speaks*, p.37.
10. Ibid, p.38.
11. Ibid, p.44.
12. Ibid, p.45.
13. Ibid, p.45.
14. *'Paul Robeson: Here I Stand', PBS American Masters, 1999.
15. Foner, Philip S., *Paul Robeson Speaks*, op. cit., p.45.

CHAPTER 28

Was Paul Racist?

Paul's father, William Drew; his Uncle Ezekiel; his Aunt Margaret; and his paternal grandparents, Benjamin and Sabra had been slaves, and there had also been a slave on his mother, Maria Louisa's side of the family. This fact had informed Paul's thinking and behaviour for the remainder of his life because, as with countless other African Americans, it was an unspeakable indignity of monumental proportions.

Paul may, therefore, be forgiven for feeling outraged at those who had enslaved what he called 'his people', and for continuing to feel bitter about the indignities that his people continued to suffer, even after the liberation of the slaves in 1865.

Clearly, races that have become distinct entities with the passage of time, develop characteristic features specific to that race. For example, one could hardly mistake a Chinese for an African. Of course, with globalisation, as the races intermarry and interbreed, such differences have tended to reduce through time.

Racism is defined as the belief that all members of each race possess characteristics, abilities, or qualities specific to that race, especially so as to distinguish as inferior or superior to another race or races.[1] This is undeniable in the case, for example, of the Inuits, who are are far more adept at surviving in cold climates than the tribes of the Amazonian rainforest. And vice versa.

However, the problem arises when the term 'racism' is used in a pejorative sense, to mean prejudice, discrimination or antagonism directed against someone of a different race, based on such a belief.[2]

Paul was, therefore, no racist in the pejorative sense. How could it be otherwise, when he had Spanish, Jewish, African American, Native American, and European blood running through his veins? Instead, he spent his life trying to *break down* barriers between different ethnic groups.

Although Paul had a natural affinity for his African American people, he supported the poor and oppressed everywhere: for example, the Welsh miners and the impoverished Chinese. And he rejoiced in what he perceived as the liberty that the Russian people had achieved by freeing themselves from the tyranny of the Czars. Although, of course, when he visited the Soviet Union, he only saw what he was permitted to see, and not that one tyranny had been replaced by another.

In the USA, the racists were, in the main, that minority of white people who continued to persecute African Americans, even after their Emancipation, and who continue to do so to this day.

1. Stevenson, A., and Waite, M., *Concise Oxford English Dictionary*.
2. Ibid.

CHAPTER 29

Paul's Forebears: Testimony of the Family

Paul spent his adult life fighting against racial inequality and social injustice. This had reached its worst excesses in the days of slavery. The fact that his forebears had been slaves, with all the cruelty and indignity which that had entailed, informed Paul's entire existence. It is, therefore, pertinent to ask what were his parents' origins? Where did his enslaved paternal grandparents live, and by whom were they enslaved? Is it possible today, one and a half centuries after black Emancipation, to find out this information?

In his autobiography, *Here I Stand* (published in 1958), said Paul, his father 'never talked with us about his early years as a slave or about his parents, Benjamin and Sabra'.[1] But Paul was aware that William Drew [and in all likelihood William's siblings, Ezekiel and Margaret] was 'born a plantation slave in Martin County, North Carolina.[2] In 1850, at about the time in question, 'the Martin County population of 8,300 included 3,500 black slaves and 320 black persons who were listed as "free"'.[3]

In her biography of her husband entitled, *Paul Robeson: Negro* (published in 1930), Eslanda stated that, 'Benjamin and Saba [i.e. Sabra] ... were slaves on the Robeson [i.e. Roberson] plantation'.[4]

Finally, Paul junior, in his biography of his father, entitled *The Undiscovered Paul Robeson*, (published in 2001), stated that William Drew 'was a field-slave on the Roberson Plantation in Robersonville in eastern North Carolina'.[5] Paul junior was correct in stating that William Drew's slave owner's surname was 'Roberson', alternatively spelt 'Robason' (but not 'Robeson', as stated by Eslanda).

A useful source of information in researching former slaves and their slave owners, is the US Federal Census, which was taken once at the beginning of each new decade from the year 1790. As a general rule, only non-enslaved persons were included in these censuses, but occasionally, the number of slaves owned by a particular slave owner was recorded.

Also, in the years 1850 and 1860, US Federal Slave Census Schedules were conducted in which the name and location of the slave owner, together with the age, gender, and colour of each of his or her slaves was recorded, but not their names.

Aside from this, the only places where slaves were mentioned by name, were in wills, family *Bibles* (where the dates of birth and death may also be mentioned), court documents, or documents appertaining to slave transactions. Otherwise, family memories or written family reminiscences have to be relied upon.

1. Robeson, Paul, with Lloyd L. Brown, *Here I Stand*, p.13.
2. Ibid, p.6.
3. Brown, Lloyd L., *The Young Paul Robeson: On My Journey Now*, p.9.
4. Robeson, Eslanda Goode, *Paul Robeson: Negro,* p.21.
5. Robeson, Paul, Jr. *The Undiscovered Paul Robeson: An Artist's Journey, 1898-1939*, p.4.

CHAPTER 30

Paul's Grandfather Benjamin who was Held in Slavery

With regard to Benjamin and his first wife, Sabra prior to Emancipation, it was illegal for enslaved persons to marry. In the era of slavery, 'Jumping the broom' was a marriage ceremony often undergone by African Americans. The ceremony had its origins in Africa. 'Brooms were waved over the heads of marrying couples', and 'the couple would often but not always jump over the broom at the end of the ceremony.'[1] No record of a marriage between Benjamin and Sabra, post-Emancipation, has been discovered.

Following Emancipation in December 1865, Benjamin adopted/used the surname of 'Congleton'. Subsequent to the death of his wife Sabra, Benjamin married Adline Goham. On the marriage licence form, dated 31 May 1889, it was stated that both Benjamin and Sabra were from Martin County, NC and that Benjamin was the son of Zibe Grice and Hannah Congleton. As for Adline, her parents were stated to be 'unknown'.[2]

When was Benjamin born? Census records indicate a birth year of 1820, but the aforesaid marriage licence form indicates a birth year of 1822. So, all that can be said is that Benjamin was born circa 1820.[3]

Nothing is known of Zibe Grice, except to say that there were no slave owners of that name in either of the adjacent counties of Pitt, Martin, or Beaufort at the estimated time of Benjamin's birth.

As for Hannah, it is virtually certain that she, and also her, son Benjamin were slaves of a person whose surname was 'Congleton'. According to the 1820 Census, there were five 'Congletons' resident in Pitt County (but none in Martin County) at the relevant time. It is, therefore, likely that Benjamin was born in Pitt County.

1. 'Jumping the Broom', *Wikipedia: The Free Encyclopedia*.
2. State of North Carolina, Martin County: Office of Register of Deeds, 31 May 1889.
3. *Ancestry*.com

CHAPTER 31

Paul's Grandmother Sabra who was Held in Slavery

When was Sabra born? Census records indicate possible birth years for Sabra variously, as 1821 or 1825. So, all that can be said is that Sabra was born circa 1823.[1]

A clue as to Sabra's ancestry is given in the 1880 Census. In that year, Anna Keel, aged 75 and described as 'mother-in-law' was living at Cross Roads Township, Martin County, NC with Benjamin Congleton as head of the household and his 'spouse', Sabra.[2]

Cross Roads Township: situated about 6 miles south-east of Robersonville.

In other words, Anna, born in 1805, was Sabra's mother. No further information has been uncovered about Anna, or her husband/spouse, except that she was born in NC.

Census records from the approximate year of Sabra's birth show that there were 9 persons by the name of 'Keels' resident in Pitt County (but none in Martin County). It is, therefore, likely that Sabra, like Benjamin, was born in Pitt County.

2. 1880 US Federal Census, *Ancestry*.
1. *Ancestry*.com

32e 'Congleton' land (to the west of route 903 and the Oak Grove Church of Christ), Pitt County, NC. Photo: Google maps.

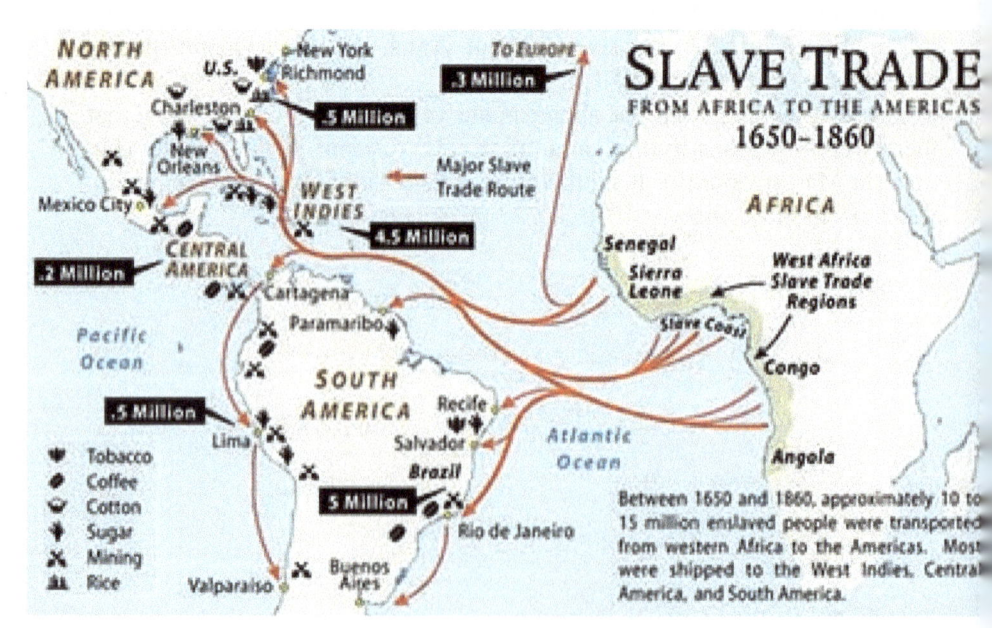

34a Slave Trade: routes from Africa to the Americas, 1650-1860. Photo: T. Bowles, printer, London.

b Map of 'Negroland', West Africa, 1729, indicating where slaves were obtained from. Photo: Herman Moll.

34c North America: East Coast. Photo: Longmans, Green, London.

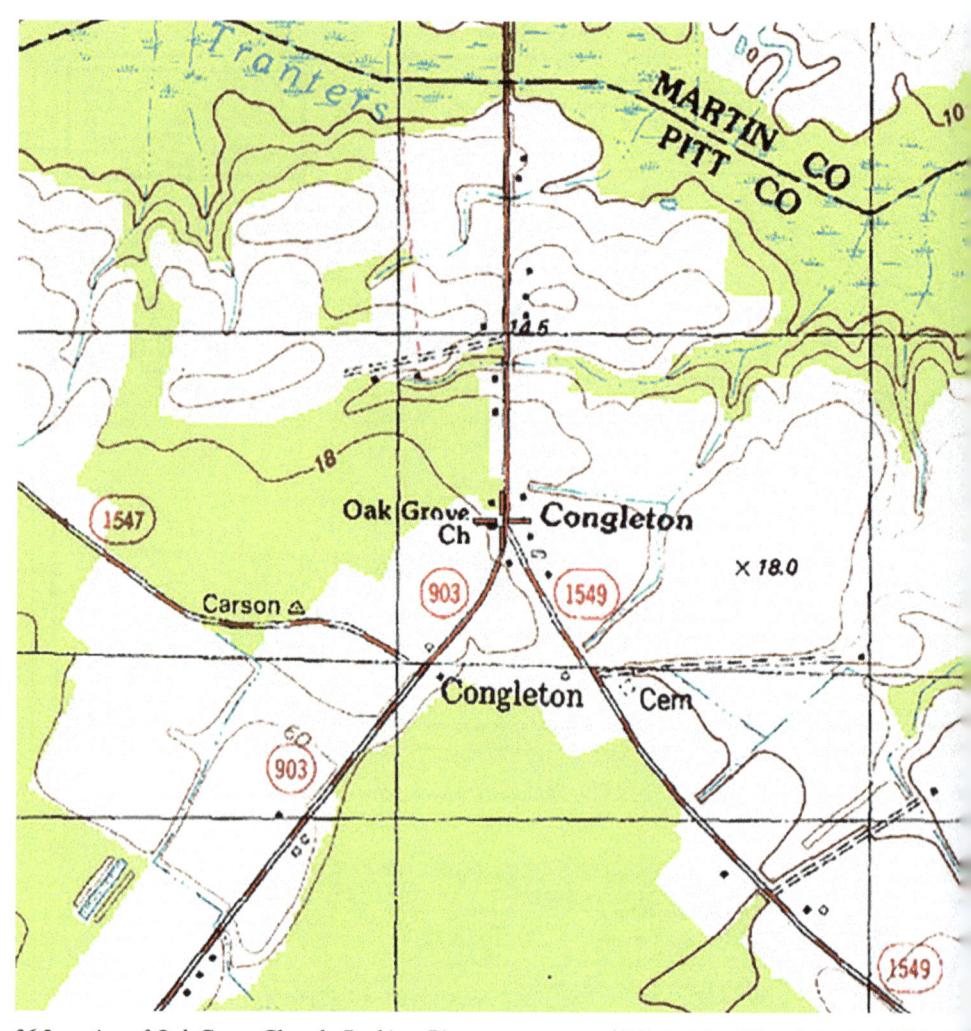

36 Location of Oak Grove Church, Perkins, Pitt County, NC in relation to the Congleton family cemetery (C). Photo: Google maps and Tammy Roberson James.

39a Location of George O. Roberson's former house (G) and his family cemetery (C), Robersonville, Martin County, NC. Photo: Google maps and Tammy Roberson James.

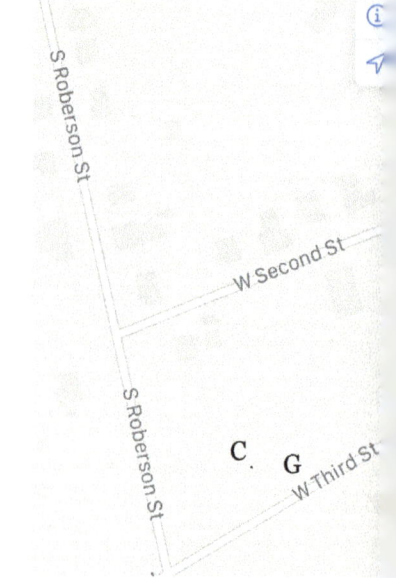

George Outlaw Roberson, his wife ewpina, and family.
oto: Tammy Roberson James.

39c The site of George O. Roberson's Plantation, Robersonville, Martin County, NC, where Sabra and her family toiled in the days of slavery.
Photo: Google maps.

42 *Harriet Tubman, c. 1868-9. Photo: Swann Galleries, NYC. Wikimedia Commons.*

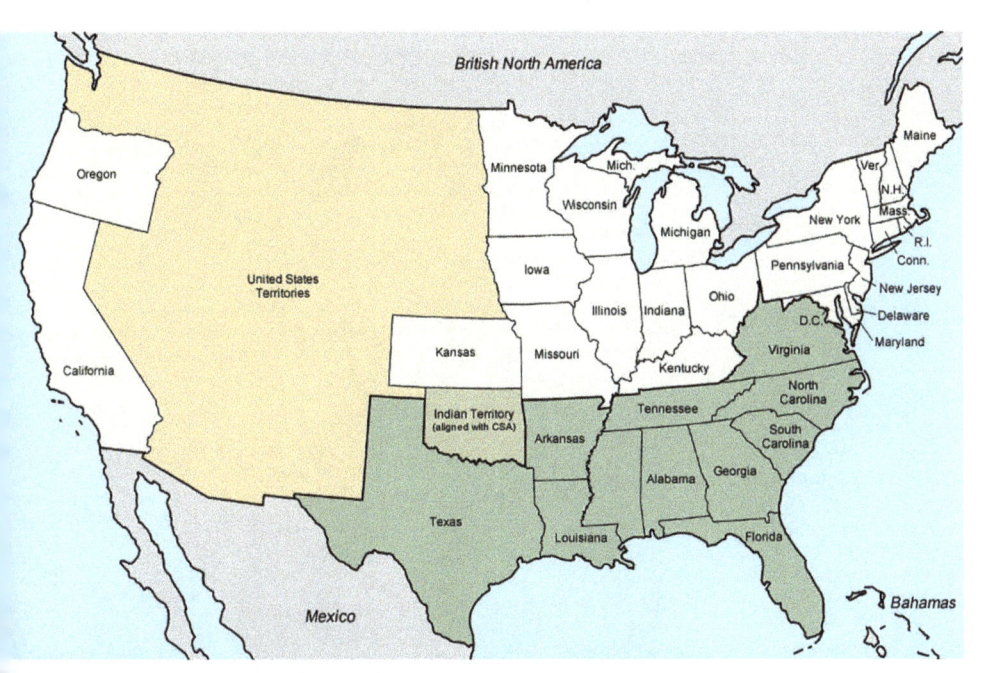

3a Free and Slave States: Tennessee joins the Confederacy, 2 July 1861.
Photo: Golbez. Wikimedia Commons.

43b Abraham Lincoln, 16th President of the USA from 1861 to 1865, showing Sojourner Truth (1797-1883) real name Isabella Baumfree, the Bible presented by the coloured people of Baltimore, Executive Mansion, Washington DC, 29 October 1864.
Photo: Library of Congress. Wikimedia Commons.

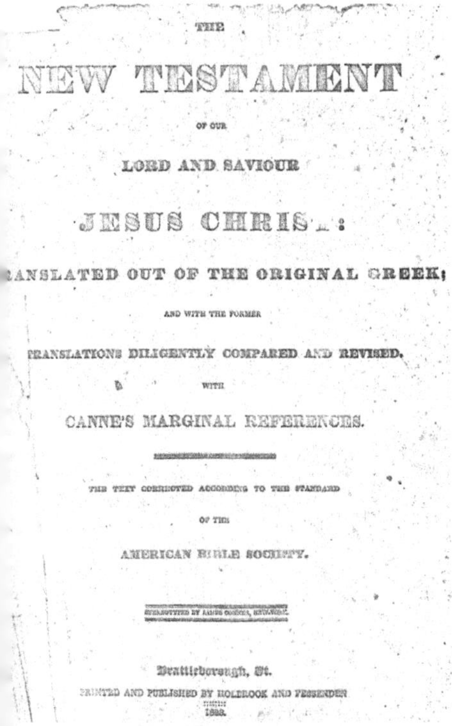

a William Roberson and his wife Sally's family ble. North Carolina State Archives.

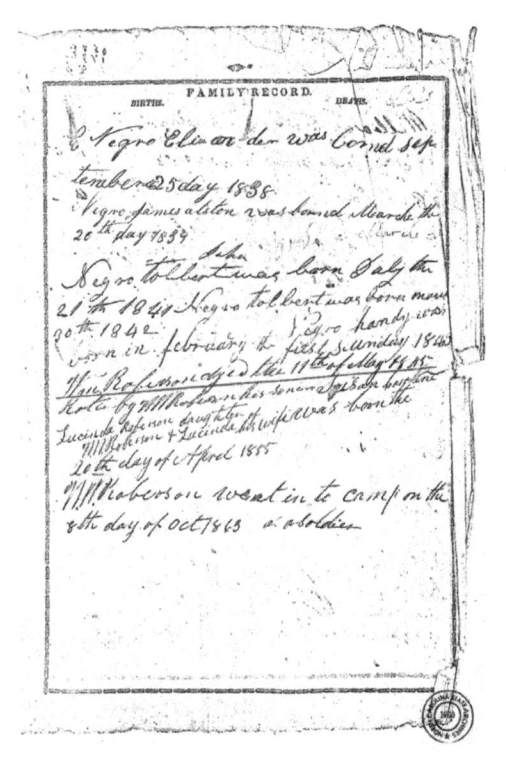

46b William Roberson and Sally's family Bible, including entries for slaves.
North Carolina State Archives.

a Charlotte Turner Bell.

PAUL ROBESON'S LAST DAYS IN PHILADELPHIA

By
Charlotte
Turner
Bell

Paul Robeson at his 75th birthday party, at 4951 Walnut Street, Philadelphia, 1973.
Photo: Paul Robeson House & Museum.

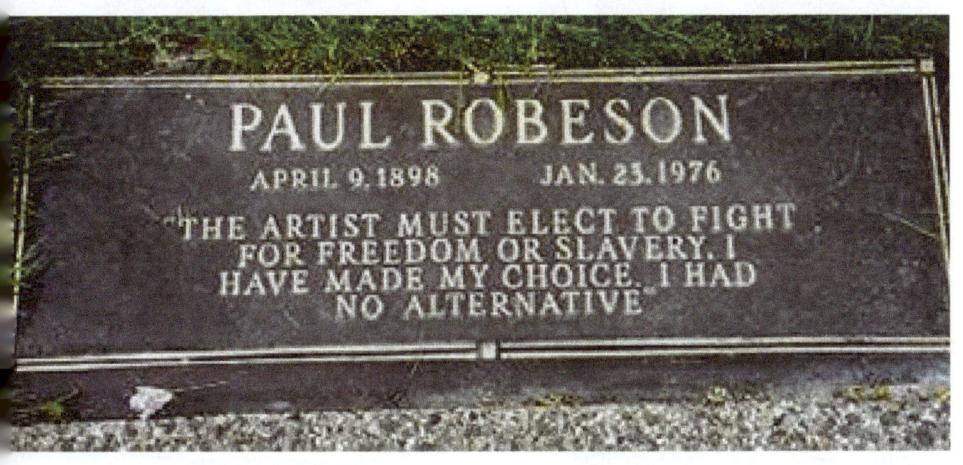

PAUL ROBESON
APRIL 9, 1898   JAN. 23, 1976

"THE ARTIST MUST ELECT TO FIGHT
FOR FREEDOM OR SLAVERY. I
HAVE MADE MY CHOICE. I HAD
NO ALTERNATIVE"

Grave of Paul Robeson, Ferncliff Cemetery and Museum, Hartsdale, Westchester County, New York.

48e Marian Forsythe and her daughter Paulina. Photo: Paul Robeson House & Museum.

Appendix 2 a Manillas from the wreck of the Douro. Photo: Terry Hiron.

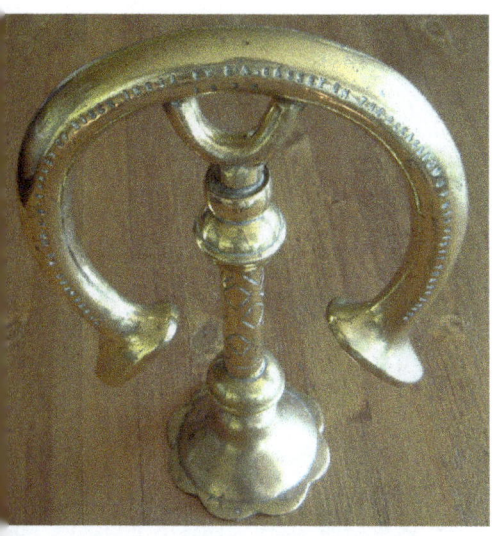

*ppendix 2 b King manilla from the wreck of
e Douro. Photo: Chris Earley.*

*ppendix 2 c Pocket watch, toasting fork, a manilla, two blue aggry and two candle-shaped aggry from
e wreck of the Douro. Photo: Terry Hiron.*

Appendix 5 a Paul Robeson House & Museum, 4951 Walnut Street, Philadelphia, 1973.
Photo: Paul Robeson House & Museum.

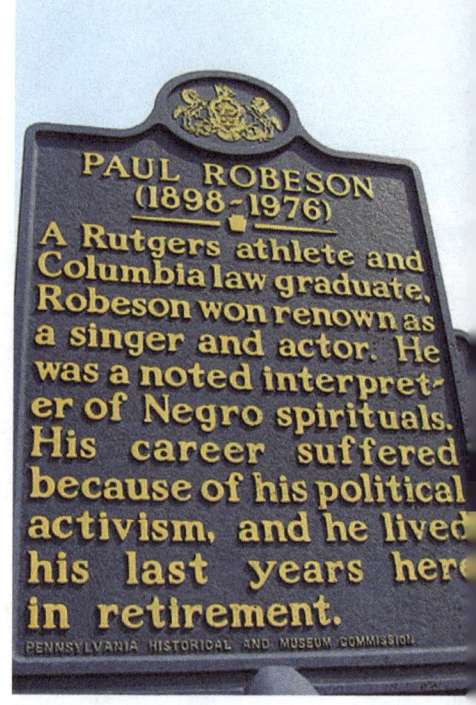

Appendix 5 b 4951 Walnut Street, Philadelphia, Plaque.

Appendix 5 c Harry Belafonte and Vernoca L. Michael, Director of the Paul Robeson House & Museum, during an event at the Robeson Center at the Brunswick campus of Rutgers University in New Jersey.
Photo: Paul Robeson House & Museum.

pendix 6 a Church of St Michael & All Angels, Steeple, Dorset, UK.

Appendix 6 c Ceiling boss, Church of St Michael & All Angels, Steeple. Courtesy, the Rector.

pendix 6 b Church of St Michael & All Angels, ^eple. Arms of the Lawrence family, quartered ^h Washington, Courtesy, the Rector.

THE DISTRICT OF COLUMBIA

WASHINGTON, D.C. 20004

WALTER E. WASHINGTON
Mayor

July 25, 1977

The Rector
Church of St. Michael
 & All Angels
Steeple, Dorset
England

Dear Rector:

We recently learned through Mr. George Honebon of Poole, that the Church of St. Michael & All Angels has an historic relationship with the family of George Washington, in whose honor our Nations Capital is named.

It was particularly interesting to see drawings of the stone armorial tablet depicting the Washington arms quartered with those of Lawrence. Because they are shown in our flag, the Washington arms are a very familiar sight in the District of Columbia.

Thinking that your parish might appreciate having some token of our mutual heritage, I have asked Mr. Honebon to carry with him on his return to England, this letter and the Flag of Washington, District of Columbia.

I know the citizens of our city join with me in this expression of friendship and best wishes to you and all the people of the community of Steeple, Dorset.

With warm personal regards.

Sincerely,

Walter E. Washington
Mayor
District of Columbia

Appendix 6 d Letter from Walter E. Washington, Mayor, District of Columbia, to the Rector of the Church of St Michael & All Angels, Steeple, Dorset, UK.
Courtesy, the Rector.

*ppendix 6 e Church of St Michael & All Angels, Steeple. Flag of Washington DC donated by Walter E. *shington, Mayor, District of Columbia. Courtesy, the Rector.

Appendix 6f Paul Robeson leading workers at the Moore Shipyard, Oakland, California in singing 'T Star-Spangled Banner', 21 September 1942.
Photo: US National Archives Records Administration. Wikimedia Commons.

Appendix 7 Tammy Roberson James with 'Grady'.    *Appendix 8 US Professor Stephen A. Bess.*

Congleton of Pitt County

Relevant Family Tree

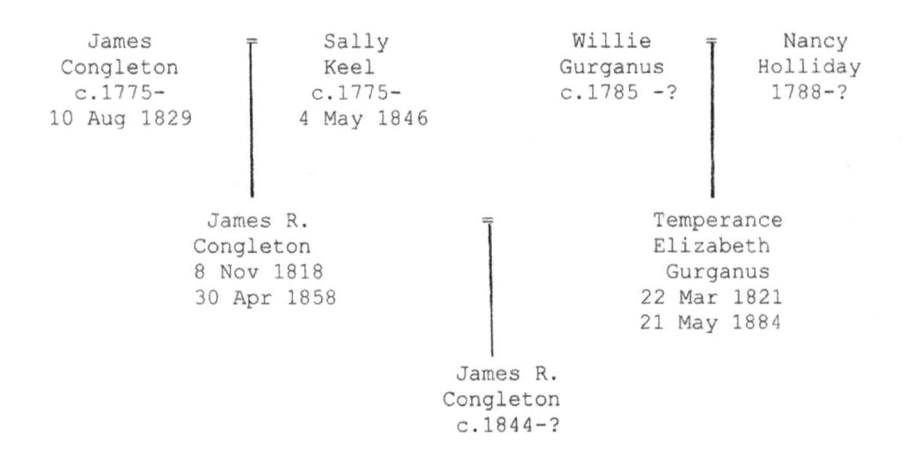

```
James            =  Sally              Willie         =  Nancy
Congleton           Keel               Gurganus          Holliday
c.1775-             c.1775-            c.1785 -?         1788-?
10 Aug 1829         4 May 1846

         James R.              =        Temperance
         Congleton                      Elizabeth
         8 Nov 1818                     Gurganus
         30 Apr 1858                    22 Mar 1821
                                        21 May 1884

                     James R.
                     Congleton
                     c.1844-?
```

Paul Robeson's Wife Eslanda

Relevant Family Tree

```
Isaac            =  Lydia
Nuñez               Weston
Carodozo            (a freed)
1793-1855           slave)

         Francis      =   Catherine
         Lewis            Romena
         Cardozo          Howell
         1838-1903        c.1841-1912

                 Eslanda        =  (1) John
                 Elbert                Jacob
                 Cardozo               Goode
                 1867-1953             1863-1901

                                =  (2) William
                                       H. Johnson

                     Eslanda        =   Paul
                     Cardozo            Leroy
                     Goode              Robeson
                     15 Dec 1895-       9 Apr 1898
                     13 Dec 1965        20 Jan 1976
```

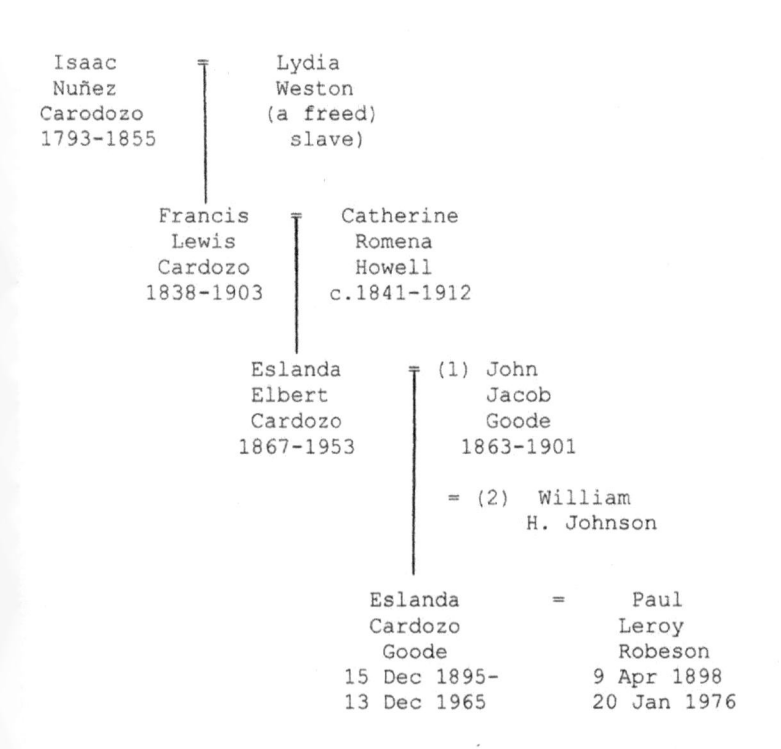

George Outlaw Roberson

Relevant Family Tree
(With number of slaves in 1790, 1850, and 1860 highlighted)

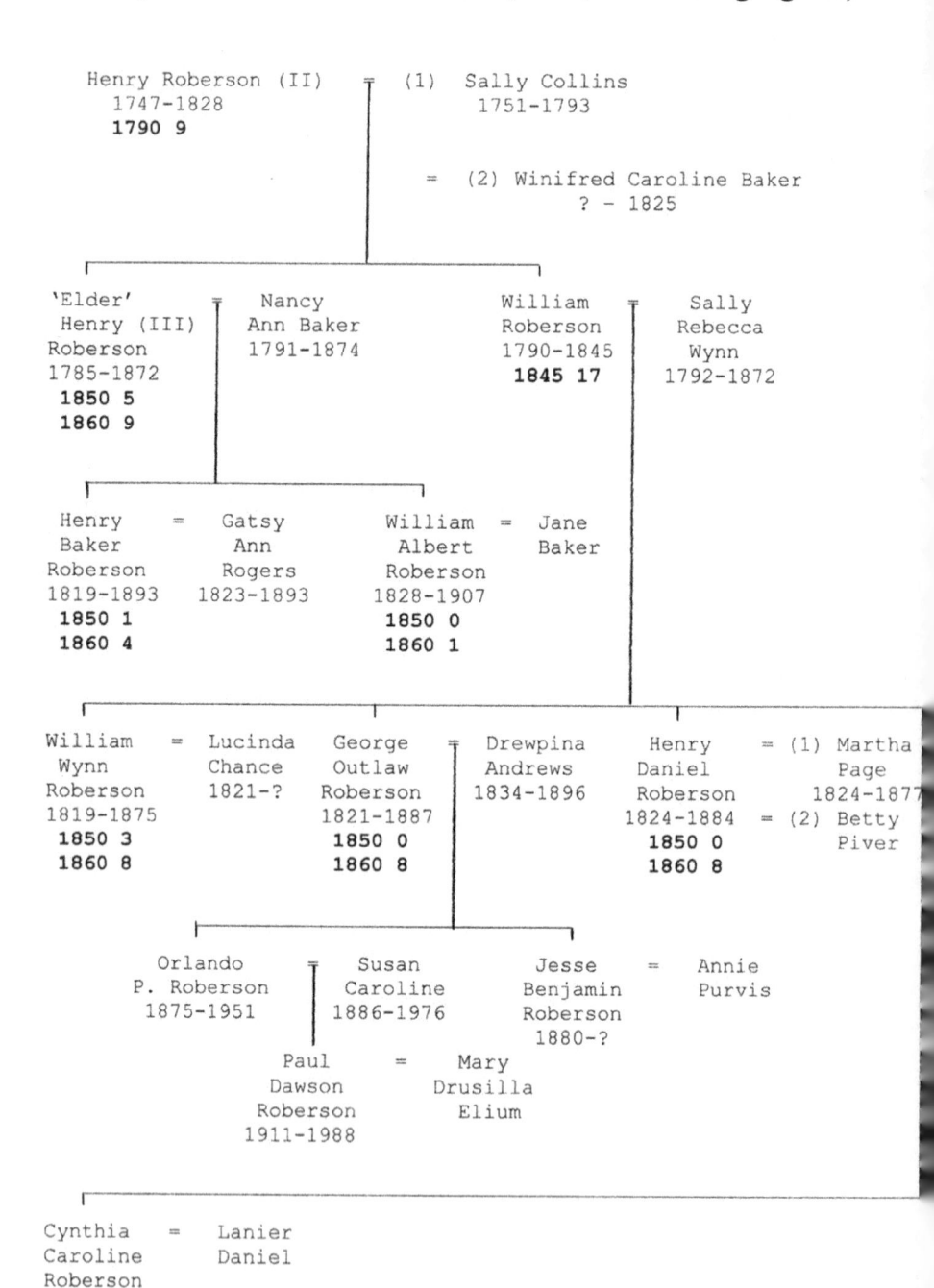

```
Henry Roberson (II)  ⊤ (1) Sally Collins
1747-1828            |      1751-1793
1790 9               |
                     |
                     = (2) Winifred Caroline Baker
                            ? - 1825
```

'Elder' Henry (III) Roberson 1785-1872 **1850 5** **1860 9** ⊤ Nancy Ann Baker 1791-1874	William Roberson 1790-1845 **1845 17** ⊤ Sally Rebecca Wynn 1792-1872

Henry Baker Roberson 1819-1893 **1850 1** **1860 4** = Gatsy Ann Rogers 1823-1893	William Albert Roberson 1828-1907 **1850 0** **1860 1** = Jane Baker

William Wynn Roberson 1819-1875 **1850 3** **1860 8** = Lucinda Chance 1821-?	George Outlaw Roberson 1821-1887 **1850 0** **1860 8** ⊤ Drewpina Andrews 1834-1896	Henry Daniel Roberson 1824-1884 **1850 0** **1860 8** = (1) Martha Page 1824-1877 = (2) Betty Piver

Orlando P. Roberson 1875-1951 ⊤ Susan Caroline 1886-1976	Jesse Benjamin Roberson 1880-? = Annie Purvis

Paul Dawson Roberson 1911-1988 = Mary Drusilla Elium

Cynthia Caroline Roberson 1838-? = Lanier Daniel

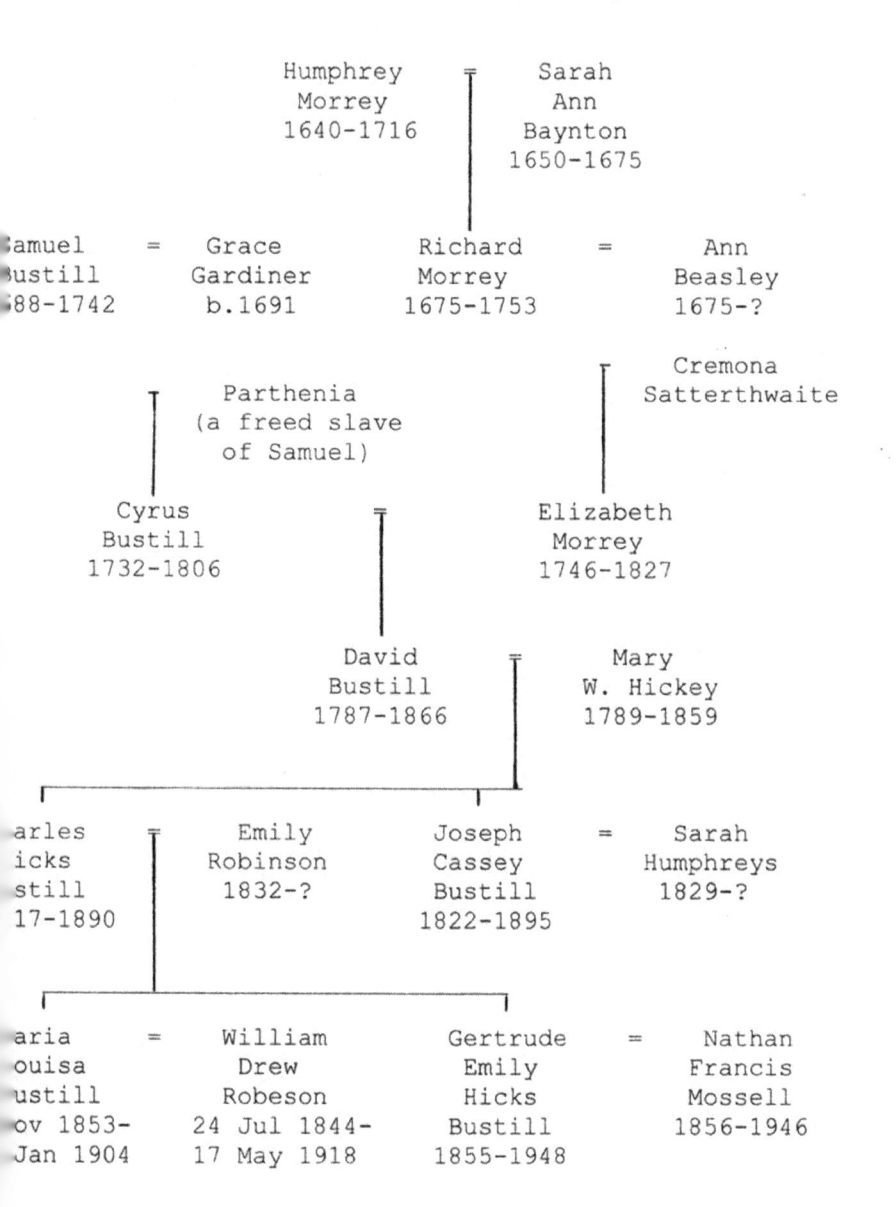

Paul Robeson

Relevant Maternal Family Tree

```
                    Humphrey  =  Sarah
                    Morrey       Ann
                    1640-1716    Baynton
                                 1650-1675
                                     |
  amuel    =  Grace         Richard      =  Ann
  ustill      Gardiner      Morrey          Beasley
  88-1742     b.1691        1675-1753       1675-?
                                               |
                                            Cremona
                 Parthenia                  Satterthwaite
                 (a freed slave                |
                  of Samuel)
     Cyrus            |              Elizabeth
     Bustill    =                    Morrey
     1732-1806        |              1746-1827
                      |
                   David       =    Mary
                   Bustill          W. Hickey
                   1787-1866        1789-1859
                      |
  ┌──────────────────┼──────────────────────┐
 arles   =  Emily         Joseph     =  Sarah
 icks       Robinson      Cassey        Humphreys
 still      1832-?        Bustill       1829-?
 17-1890                  1822-1895
     |
  ┌──────────────┬──────────────────────┐
 aria    =  William       Gertrude   =  Nathan
 ouisa      Drew          Emily         Francis
 ustill     Robeson       Hicks         Mossell
 ov 1853-   24 Jul 1844-  Bustill       1856-1946
 Jan 1904   17 May 1918   1855-1948
```

Paul Robeson

Relevant Paternal Family Tree

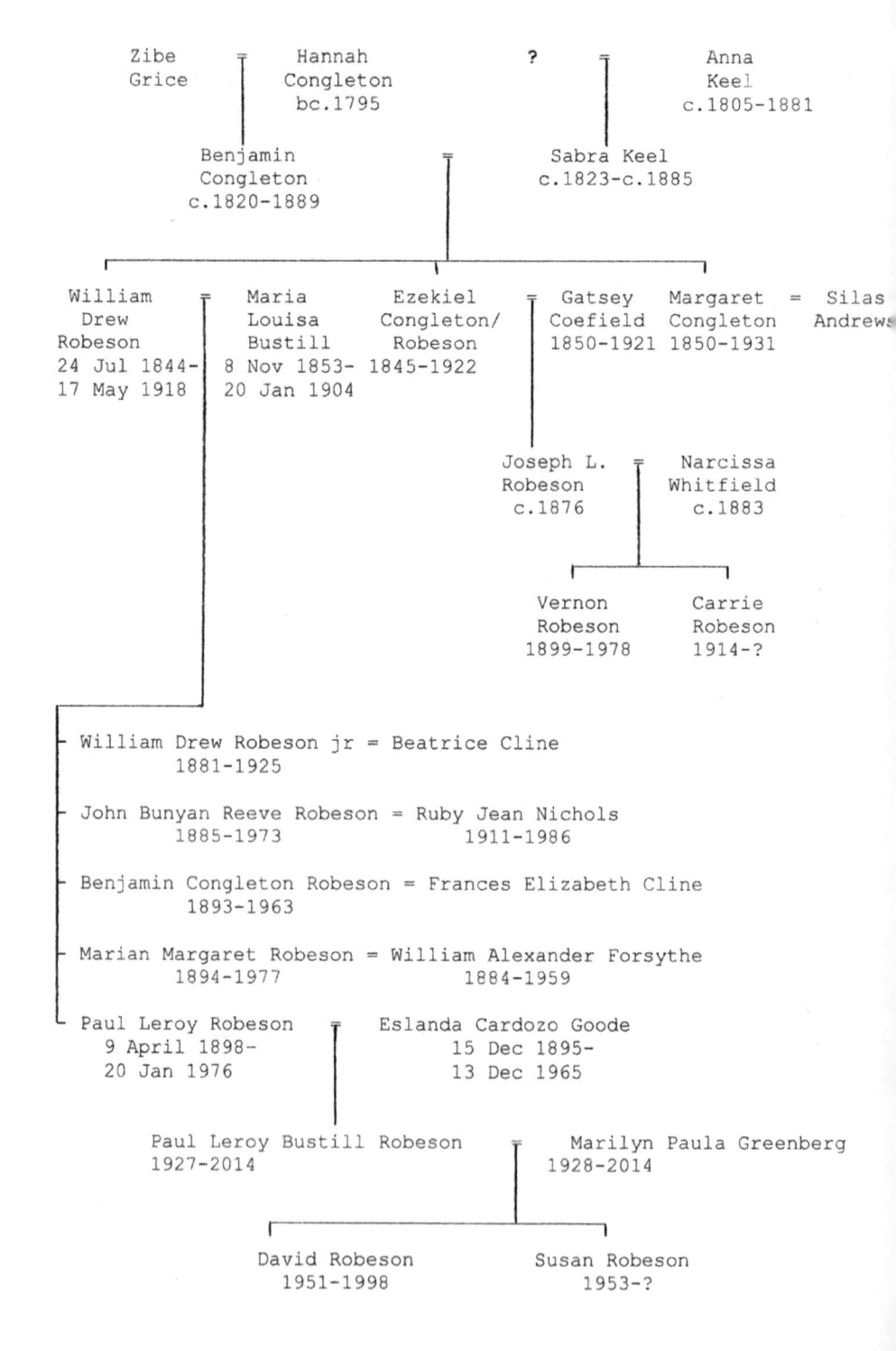

```
    Zibe      =  Hannah              ?      =    Anna
    Grice        Congleton                       Keel
                 bc.1795                         c.1805-1881

           Benjamin           =      Sabra Keel
           Congleton                 c.1823-c.1885
           c.1820-1889


William   =  Maria      Ezekiel      =  Gatsey      Margaret   =  Silas
Drew         Louisa     Congleton/      Coefield    Congleton     Andrews
Robeson      Bustill    Robeson         1850-1921   1850-1931
24 Jul 1844- 8 Nov 1853-1845-1922
17 May 1918  20 Jan 1904

                              Joseph L.    =  Narcissa
                              Robeson         Whitfield
                              c.1876          c.1883

                              Vernon          Carrie
                              Robeson         Robeson
                              1899-1978       1914-?
```

- William Drew Robeson jr = Beatrice Cline
    1881-1925

- John Bunyan Reeve Robeson = Ruby Jean Nichols
    1885-1973   1911-1986

- Benjamin Congleton Robeson = Frances Elizabeth Cline
    1893-1963

- Marian Margaret Robeson = William Alexander Forsythe
    1894-1977   1884-1959

- Paul Leroy Robeson   = Eslanda Cardozo Goode
    9 April 1898-   15 Dec 1895-
    20 Jan 1976   13 Dec 1965

        Paul Leroy Bustill Robeson   =   Marilyn Paula Greenberg
        1927-2014   1928-2014

              David Robeson   Susan Robeson
              1951-1998   1953-?

CHAPTER 32

Temperance Congleton: A Link with the Robersons

Given the fact that following Emancipation slaves, for identification purposes, frequently adopted the name of their last slave owner, the question arises, was there any slave owner named 'Congleton' who was resident in Pitt County during the later years of slavery? Yes, in 1860, there was one slave owner of that name: Temperance Congleton, who was the owner of 14 slaves. (There were no 'Congleton' slave owners in Martin County in 1860.)

Temperance Elizabeth Congleton (née Gurganus) was born on 22 March 1821. She was the widow of James R. Congleton, who died on 30 April 1858. She had borne him 7 children: 5 boys and 2 girls. According to the Slave Census in 1850, James ('Jas') R. Congleton had owned 7 slaves. The Congletons had their origins in the British Isles.

CHAPTER 33

The Geographical Proximity of the Roberson and Congleton Families

Robersonville in Martin County, where Sabra and her children were slaves, is situated a mere 5 miles from the border with Pitt County. The question now is, where was the Congleton's homestead [or 'homeplace'] and plantation situated?

From a 'deed abstract' diagram from the *Pitt County Deed Book*, dated November 1773,[1] and from other sources, it is deduced that the Congleton land was located to the north-east of the town of Stokes, Pitt County, and adjacent to the border with Martin County. As regards the Congleton homestead, it is reasonable to suppose that this was in the vicinity of the small, eponymous settlement of 'Congleton'. Finally, Congleton is a mere 5½ miles from Robersonville.

1. *Pitt County Deed Book F*, November 1773, p.3, William Congleton to Abraham Congleton, Courtesy William Kittrell.

CHAPTER 34

From what Region of Africa did Benjamin and Sabra's Forebears Originate?

Between 1650 and 1860, some 10 to 15 million people from West Africa were enslaved and transported to foreign lands. Of these, some 0.5 million were shipped to North America, principally by Great Britain.

London cartographer, engraver, and publisher, Herman Moll's 1729 map depicts two vast regions of West Africa: namely, 'Negroland' lying south of the Sahara Desert, and the coastal region of 'Guinea' lying south of Negroland. (Today, 'Guinea' corresponds to the countries stretching from Guinea in the west to Nigeria in the east.) Furthermore, Moll divided Guinea into three regions: the one to the east being the 'Slave Coast', suggesting that this is where slaves were assembled prior to transportation. The 'Slave Coast' corresponds approximately with present day Nigeria, and it is likely that Benjamin and Sabra's forebears came from this region of West Africa.

Local black tribal rulers were complicit in the slave trade, and in the early years, the slaves put up for sale by them were prisoners of war. They would be taken to a series of forts, of which more than thirty dotted the West African coast.

What did the tribal leaders require in return for slaves and other merchandise? The answer - guns, ammunition and powder, which they needed to fight wars and to protect their own people.

CHAPTER 35

How and Where did Benjamin and Sabra First Meet?

Given the fact that Benjamin was a slave of the Congletons in Pitt County, and Sabra was a slave of the Robersons in Martin County, how did they first meet?

They may have encountered one another at a slave gathering: such social events being encouraged from time to time, by the slave owners in order to avoid discontent.

Or, Benjamin may have been deliberately introduced to Sabra for the purpose of procreation, assuming, of course, that they were both healthy and strong. The reason for this was twofold: in order to increase the slave population (thereby avoiding the necessity of the slave owner having to purchase more slaves), and also to improve the quality of the stock, by eugenics.

Eugenics: using controlled breeding to increase the occurrence of desirable heritable characteristics in a population.[1]

Or, Benjamin may have been on loan or hire to the Robersons of Martin County at the time. Lastly, they may have met in church.

1. Stevenson, A., and Waite, M., *Concise Oxford English Dictionary*.

CHAPTER 36

Oak Grove Church, Perkins, Pitt County, North Carolina: A Congleton-Roberson Connection

Oak Grove Primitive Baptist Church in Perkins Township, Pitt County is situated only about 6 miles from Robersonville in Martin County. Furthermore, both the Robersons and the Congletons had associations with Oak Grove Church.

On 3 November 1848, Oak Grove Church became affiliated to the Disciples of Christ.[5] This was a Protestant denomination, originating among American Presbyterians in the early 19th century and found chiefly in the US: it rejects creeds and regards the *Bible* as the only basis of faith.[6]

Furthermore, 'Elder' Henry Roberson, whose home was situated about 2 miles south of Robersonville, was enrolled on that date as a preacher at the aforesaid church.[4]

Were James R. Congleton and his wife, Temperance members of the Disciples of Christ Church, and therefore members of Elder Henry's congregation at Oak Grove Church? The answer is yes. Temperance died at her home in Carolina Township, Pitt County on 21 May 1884. Her death was reported by the *Eastern Reflector* with the words, 'she was a member of the Disciples Church'. So, presumably, the late James and their offspring had likewise been members.[7]

Benjamin, as a slave of the Congletons and Sabra, as a slave of the Robersons were undoubtedly baptised into the Christian faith, and they may both have been permitted to attend Oak Grove Church on Sundays, albeit separated from the 'white' members of the congregation, and this may have been where they first met. (Black people were encouraged to attend church in order to instil into them the notion that to be obedient to their master was God's will, and to do otherwise was to be sinful.)

1. Ware, Charles Crossfield, *North Carolina Disciples of Christ*, p.253.
2. Stevenson, A., and Waite, M., *Concise Oxford English Dictionary*.
3. Ware, Charles Crossfield (editor), *Tar Heel Disciples, 1841-1852*, (New Bern, North Carolina, 1942).
4. Our Family Tree: Branch: Ray's Extended Family Tree', ourfamtree.org

CHAPTER 37

Benjamin as a Slave for Hire

The Guardian Returns 'of the Estate of James R. Congleton decd [deceased]', who died on 30 April 1858, have been preserved.
Guardian Returns: the accounts of a person who is legally responsible for someone unable to manage their own affairs:[1] in this case James's widow, Temperance.

They contain the following information:

'1 Negro Ben hired to Ilie [Willie] Gurganus for 1858 - $70.00.
One boy Ben hired to John L. Ross for the year 1859 - $115.00.
One boy Ben hired to John Leggett for the year of 1861 - $100.00.
Negro hire[d] for 1863 Ben to Samuel Keel - $100.00.
Negro hired[d] for the [year] 1864, Ben to Josiah Taylor - $350.'[2]

It seems likely that 'Negro Ben' and 'Boy Ben' were one and the same person, and that person was Benjamin Congleton.
As previously mentioned, Eslanda stated that, 'Benjamin and Saba [i.e. Sabra] ... were slaves on the Robeson [Roberson] plantation' in Martin County, North Carolina.[3] If this is correct, it implies that at some time prior to Emancipation, Benjamin had been hired out to the Robersons by the Congletons.

1. Stevenson, A., and Waite, M., *Concise Oxford English Dictionary*.
2. Cron, Frederick H. and Fred W. Harrison, 'In Loving Remembrance of Sabra Robeson'.
3. Robeson, Eslanda Goode, *Paul Robeson: Negro*, p.21.

CHAPTER 38

The Birth of William Drew, Ezekiel, and Margaret

Paul stated that his father, William Drew Robeson had been 'born a plantation slave' in Martin County, NC. As for the location, Paul stated that William Drew, 'was born in 1843 in eastern North Carolina near Rocky Mount'.[1]

Rocky Mount: situated some 35 miles to the west of Robersonville.

However, this is unlikely because, according to the Slave Schedules for 1850 and 1860, there were no Robason/Roberson slave owners living in the vicinity of Rocky Mount at that time. However, there were slave owners by the name of 'Robason' living in Martin County in both 1850 and 1860.

Paul junior stated that William Drew was a slave 'on the Roberson Plantation in Robersonville' NC, where there *were* slave owners named 'Roberson' at the relevant time. It is probably the case, therefore, that William's siblings, Ezekiel and Margaret were also born at the same location. But when?

William Drew: Paul's wife Eslanda ('Essie') gave William Drew's date of birth as 27 July 1845.[2] But Paul gave two conflicting dates: the year 1843 (as above), and the year 1845 ('My father escaped at the age of fifteen in 1860'[3]). However, Stephen A. Bess is clear that William Drew was born on 24 July 1844.[4]

Ezekiel: In the 1870 Census, Ezekiel Congleton's age is given as 30, which would indicate a birth year 1840. However, in 1920 Census, Ezekiel Robeson (the surname he was now using)'s age is given as 73, indicating a birth year of 1847. Finally, Paul junior stated that William Drew escaped 'with his older brother Ezekiel'.[5] However, Stephen A. Bess is clear that Ezekiel, who was his great-grandfather x2, was the *younger* brother of William Drew, and that Ezekiel was born in 1845.[6]

Margaret: On Margaret's death certificate (she died on 29 January 1931) her age is stated as 'Near 81', indicating that she was born in the year 1850. However, in the 1870 Census, an age of 25 is given, indicating that she was born in 1845. Finally, in the 1900 Census, where Margaret and Silas, a farmer, are living at Bear Grass, Martin, NC her month and year of birth are given as July 1850. This tallies with the death certificate year and may therefore be taken as accurate. Interestingly, neither Silas nor Margaret could read or write.

Also, on Margaret's death certificate, her father's name was given as Benjamin Congleton, but after 'Mother', the entry was 'don't know'. This suggests that Sabra was not her mother. Perhaps this is why neither Paul, Eslanda, nor their son Paul junior mention Margaret in their various accounts.

Benjamin and Sabra could only have dreamed that one day the whole family would be free. They would never have dreamed, that in the fullness of time, William Drew would father a son, who would become famous the world over!

1. Robeson, Paul, 'Here's My Story', *Freedom*, Volume I, Number 1, January 1951.
2. Robeson, Eslanda Goode, *Paul Robeson: Negro*, p.21.
3. Robeson, Paul, with Lloyd L. Brown, *Here I Stand*, p.6.
4. Stephen A. Bess, personal communication to the author, 23 December 2020.
5. Robeson, Paul, Jr., *The Undiscovered Paul Robeson: An Artist's Journey, 1898-1939*, p.4.
6. Stephen A. Bess, personal communication to the author, to the author, 23 December 2020.

CHAPTER 39

The Identity of the Slave Owner of Sabra and her children

A Challenge! Is it possible today, 16 decades after Emancipation, to discover the name and abode of the slave owner of Paul's father, William Drew Robeson and his mother and siblings?

The Slave Schedule for 1860, taken 5 years before Emancipation in December 1865, records six possible 'Roberson' slave owners in the vicinity of Robersonville, all of whom were members of a close-knit family. But which of these 6 was the slave owner in question?

A clue was provided by Paul himself, in his autobiography *Here I Stand*. One evening in New York, he said:

'I had gone to a downtown nightclub to hear a friend who was singing in the place, and there I was accosted by a man who introduced himself as one of the Robesons [i.e. Robersons] of North Carolina. He said he was sure that I'd be pleased to hear that his mother was quite proud of my accomplishments in life, and that she had carefully kept a scrapbook on the various honors that I had won for the family name. Then the stranger went on to say that he would like to get together with me for a chat someday soon. "You see", he confided proudly, "your father used to work for my grandfather". As politely as was possible under the circumstances I assured the Southern gentleman that it was undoubtedly true that the Negroes who had come by his family's name had added a bit more distinction to it than did any of the original owners or their descendants. "You say my father 'used to work' for your grandfather. Let's put it the way it was: *Your grandfather exploited my father as a slave!*" - That ended it; and *this* Robeson never did have a chummy get together with *that* one.'[1]

Who was this man whom Paul had put so firmly in his place, and who was his grandfather? It remained for Lloyd L. Brown to solve the final mystery. Lloyd Louis Brown (1913-2003) was an African American US labour organizer, Communist Party activist, journalist, writer, and editor.

Paul's friend for 25 years, Brown collaborated with him on the writing of his autobiography, and on numerous other of his writings.[2]

In his biography of Paul, entitled *The Young Paul Robeson: On My Journey Now* (published in 1997), Brown described a meeting between himself and white attorney, Paul D. [Dawson] Roberson: 'a short, thin, sharp-faced man of sixty whose grandfather George O. [Outlaw] Robason was one of the three founders of Robersonville'. Said Brown, 'He declined to shake my hand when I visited him at his Railroad Street office [Robersonville] (too much social equality, perhaps), but he was helpful nevertheless in providing the names and addresses of two of Paul's relatives. He was very guarded in talking about his connection with the Robeson I was concerned with, observing that he had admired the famous athlete, actor, and singer, "before he turned pink"'.

'Pinko': a person with left-wing or liberal views.[3]

'From other sources', Brown continued, 'I had reason to believe that Paul Roberson's grandfather had been the slave owner from whom [Paul's father] William [Drew] Robeson escaped'. Moreover, 'when Attorney Roberson told me that he had been in New York when Paul Robeson was playing in *Othello*, I was certain that he was the man of whom Paul had written in *Here I Stand*'.[4]

1. Robeson, Paul, with Lloyd L. Brown, *Here I Stand*, p.14.
2. Lloyd L. Brown wrote for *Freedom* (1951-55), 'a newspaper founded in Harlem, New York by activists Paul Robeson and Louis Burnham during the Cold War and McCarthy eras. It openly challenged racism, imperialism, colonialism, and political repression and advocated for civil rights, labor rights and world peace'.
2. NYU Digital Library.
3. Stevenson, A., and Waite, M., *Concise Oxford English Dictionary*.
4. Brown, Lloyd L., *The Young Paul Robeson: On My Journey Now*, pp.139-140.

CHAPTER 40

More About George Outlaw Roberson

George Outlaw Roberson of Robersonville, North Carolina was the son of William Roberson and his wife, Sally Rebecca (née Wynn). ('Outlaw', the name used in his family's *Bible*, is sometimes spelt 'Outler'.)

From deeds and other records, it is known that George O. Roberson (and his father before him) 'operated a general merchandise store and furnished farm supplies. The store was located on the north-west corner of what is now known as Railroad and Roberson Streets. Along from the house to his store was located the harness shop, blacksmith shop, cotton gin [machine for separating cotton from its seeds], slave quarters, wine press, distillery, and barns.'[1] It is probable that Sabra and her children occupied these very 'slave quarters' and picked some of the cotton referred to above.

'Prior to and after the Civil War', George was also a 'commission merchant', who 'hauled the cotton to Hamilton, NC, where it was shipped [down the Roanoke River] to Baltimore, Maryland and occasionally to Philadelphia, Pennsylvania'.[2]

'There were many apple orchards' in the vicinity of George's homestead, 'which we are led to believe must have been of high quality. Apple trees within the town ... provided the fruit for the brandy'.[3]

George's 'homeplace', which was built about 1857, was located on Third Street, Robersonville. (The homestead was demolished in the 1980s.) Adjoining its grounds was the Roberson family cemetery. On 20 October of that year George married Drewpina Andrews. She bore him eight sons and one daughter.[4]

George's plantation lay to the west of Robersonville, and this is undoubtedly where William Drew and Ezekiel toiled as slaves (and possibly Sabra and Margaret also, though their duties may well have been confined to their master George's house).

On 23 July 1863, the second year of the Civil War, George enlisted in the Confederate Army. When he returned from the war, 'he built a store of his own, across the road from the original store'.[5]

In 1872, the town of Robersonville, which was named after George and his two brothers William and Henry, was incorporated.

George O. Roberson died on 27 August 1887. His wife Drewpina died on 18 October 1896.

When I contacted George's great-granddaughter x2, Tammy Roberson James, of Robersonville, to my amazement she produced a group photograph, of George, his wife, Drewpina, and two of their children! This is one of the earliest photographs ever taken in North Carolina.

In the Roberson family cemetery, some graves lie out in the open and others are almost hidden by trees. Many of the headstones are broken and scattered about. However, on one, it is possible to make out an inscription, 'Caroline', followed by the letter 'D'.[6] This was the grave of George's eldest sister (Cynthia) Caroline Roberson (born 23 June 1838), who married Lanier Daniel. It is therefore virtually certain, that this is where George and his wife, Drewpina are buried.

Sadly, the final resting place of Benjamin and Sabra have not been identified, but it is likely that they were both buried at Cross Roads Township, Martin County.

1. Hughes, Jean Nelson (editor), *Martin County Heritage*, p.509.
2. Ibid, p.509.
3. Ibid, p.509.
4. Ibid, p.509.
5. Ibid, p.503.
6. Tammy Roberson James, personal communication to the author, 29 September 2020.

CHAPTER 41

The Escape of William Drew, Ezekiel, and Margaret

According to Paul, his father William Drew 'escaped at the age of 15 in 1860', and according to Paul junior, William Drew 'escaped with his older [in fact, younger] brother' to Pennsylvania. It is likely that Margaret escaped at the same time. If true, this was prior to the outbreak of the American Civil War, which commenced on 12 April 1861.

Abraham Lincoln, who was elected President of the United States in November 1860, was known to be an opponent of slavery. Almost immediately, South Carolina seceded from the Union, followed shortly afterwards by 10 other states. These 11 states formed the Confederate States of America early in 1861 (otherwise known as 'The Confederacy', or 'The South'), which, in the ensuing Civil War, were ranged against the forces of 'The Union' (or 'The North').

Paul's father, William Drew never discussed his early years as a slave. Had he done so, said Paul, 'I'm sure that had he ever spoken about this part of his life it would have been utterly impossible for me as a boy to grasp the idea that a noble human being like my father had actually been owned by another man – to be bought and sold, used and abused at will'.[1]

However, Paul 'learned from others' that 'Pop made at least one, and possibly two, dangerous trips back to the plantation to see her [Sabra]'.[2] This was in order 'to carry money to the mother he loved so dearly'. William Drew had earned the money by working on farms.[3] And this, said Paul junior, was 'despite extreme hazards'.[4]

When the Civil War began, said Paul junior, William Drew and Ezekiel 'joined a Union Army labor battalion that ultimately accompanied the advancing Union troops in 1864'.[5] In fact, the name 'Ezekiel Robeson' (spelt 'Robrson') appears in the Georgia Civil War Muster Rolls, January 1864, as a member of the 'Seventeenth Senatorial District Burke County, Military Company, District Number 6'.[6]

Said Paul junior, 'According to family legend, the two brothers took up arms, along with others in the battalion, to repel a surprise attack by the

Confederate, General George Pickett on the Union-occupied city of New Bern, North Carolina'.[7] New Bern, Craven County, NC, is situated about 65 miles south of Robersonville. However, the evidence is that only Ezekiel, and not William Drew, was a combatant.

The Battle of New Bern was fought on 14 March 1862. The Union Army was victorious and New Bern remained under Union for the rest of the war. Said Lloyd L. Brown, 'within three months some 7,500 runaways had arrived there'.[8]

Said Brown, Ezekiel, 'told his grandson, Vernon Roberson, that when the Yankee army took New Bern, he was one of those who took off to join them there. Vernon Roberson (1899-1978) was the son of Ezekiel's son, Joseph L. Roberson (born 1876) and his wife, Narcissa (née Whitfield). This implies that Ezekiel and his siblings had, in fact, escaped 11 months *after* the commencement of the Civil War, and not, as Paul had suggested, in 1860, prior to the onset of the war.

Finally, Brown described how he had met Vernon Roberson and Vernon's sister, Mrs Carrie Lloyd who were Ezekiel's grandchildren. 'They told me that Ezekiel, who lived until the 1920s, had talked with them about the escape of the younger enslaved Robersons [i.e. William Drew and Ezekiel] had made to the Yankees at New Bern'.[9]

Yankee: an inhabitant of New England (comprising Maine; Vermont; Massachusetts; Connecticut; Rhode Island; New Hampshire) or of one of the northern states.[10]

William Drew was listed on the payroll of Captain William Holden, quartermaster at New Bern. 'In all likelihood', said Brown, William Drew 'was one of the hundreds of black fugitives who were hired by the Union Army to build fortifications and to work as woodcutters, teamsters [drivers of teams of animals], longshoremen, cooks, and laundresses'.[11] For this, they 'were paid $10 a month'. 'Probably William was a teamster, for in later life he would show a proficiency in handling horses'.[12]

Margaret also escaped to New Bern, said Lloyd L. Brown, where she 'was paid $10 for the month of January 1865 as one of several women cooks in the [Union] Army camps for the contrabands'.[13]

'In this region nearly 10,000 enslaved Blacks escaped during this period and went to the Union camps for protection and freedom. The Union army organized the adults for work; missionaries came to teach literacy to both adults and children.'[14] Therefore, having escaped from slavery with presumably a minimal education and the inability to read or write, William Drew, Ezekiel, and Margaret would have been given the opportunity to become literate.

1. Robeson, Paul, with Lloyd L. Brown, *Here I Stand*, pp.13-14.
2. Ibid, pp.13-14.
3. Robeson, Paul, 'Here's My Story by Paul Robeson', *Freedom*, Volume I, Number 1, January 1951.
4. Robeson, Paul, Jr., *The Undiscovered Paul Robeson: An Artist's Journey, 1898-1939*, p.4.
5. Ibid, p.4.
6. Civil War Muster Rolls, *Ancestry.com*
7. Robeson Jr., Paul (2001). *The Undiscovered Paul Robeson: An Artist's Journey*, op. cit., p.4
8. Brown, Lloyd L., *The Young Paul Robeson: On My Journey Now*, p.12.
9. Ibid, p.140.
10. Stevenson, A., and Waite, M., *Concise Oxford English Dictionary*.
11. Brown, Lloyd L., *The Young Paul Robeson: On My Journey Now*, op. cit., p.12.
12. Ibid, p.13.
13. Kimball, A. S., 'Skilled Laborers', *Report of Persons and Articles Hired, New Bern, N.C.*, January-April 1865, in Lloyd L. Brown, p.14.
14. *Wikipedia*.

CHAPTER 42

How did William Drew, Ezekiel, and Margaret Effect their Escape? The 'Underground Railroad'

In 1787, US abolitionist and Quaker, Isaac Tatem Hopper began to organize a network of secret routes, secret agents, and safe houses in order to facilitate the escape of fugitive slaves to the slave-free states and Canada. 'An estimated 30,000 to 100,000 slaves escaped via the euphemistically named 'Underground Railroad' which 'reached its height between 1810 and 1850'.[1]

Not only Quakers (Members of the Religious Society of Friends), but also Baptists, Methodists and other religious sects helped in operating the Underground Railroad. Even some judges and attorneys were abolitionists who helped slaves to escape. Some clergymen allowed the bell towers of their churches to be used as places of refuge for those slaves who were in transit. Those who hosted fugitives in their homes and arranged safe passage to freedom were known as 'Station Masters'.[2]

Harriet Tubman (c.1821-1913), a black woman, 'was the legendary "conductor" on the Underground Railroad. She was called 'Moses' by the slaves who followed her north to freedom'.

'Conductor': a person who led missions to rescue slaves.

Moses (c.14-13 centuries BCE): Hebrew prophet and lawgiver, born in Egypt, and led the Israelites away from servitude there, across the desert towards the Promised Land.[3]

Born a slave on the eastern shore of Maryland, Harriet escaped from slavery 'when nearly thirty years of age and devoted herself to guiding others to freedom. She made nineteen journeys into slave territory during a period of ten years, and brought back more than three hundred men, women, and children'.[4]

Said Paul, 'When Harriet Tubman [showing enormous courage] went South in the dark days to lead the slaves and perhaps, my father by way of the Underground Railway [Railroad] to freedom, thousands of human beings — the "salt of the earth" — lifted their voices in song. And so it has been wherever those of human kind have surged toward the light of liberation — men and women of every culture, color and clime'.[5]

131

Without the assistance of the Underground Railroad, it would have been virtually impossible for a slave to escape. The terrain of North Carolina was environmentally hostile, with dense forests, rattlesnakes, copperhead snakes, and water moccasins snakes, wild boar, wolves, and coyotes, swamps, great rivers, and alligators. And, of course, the white slave owners were always on the lookout and ready to apprehend the escaping slave and return him or her to their slave master.

Likewise, it can safely be be said that without the help of the Underground Railroad, escape for William Drew, Ezekiel, and Margaret would not have been possible.

1. 'The Underground Railroad and How it Began', Dummies, online.
2. 'Underground Railroad', *Wikipedia*
3. Stevenson, A., and Waite, M., *Concise Oxford English Dictionary*.
4. Foner, Philip S., *Paul Robeson Speaks*, op. cit., p.517.
5. Robeson, Paul, *The Second People's Song Book*.

CHAPTER 43

The American Civil War (12 April 1861 to 9 May 1865): The Contribution made by Blacks

For the North, both northern free Blacks, and southern runaway slaves (including Ezekiel, as a combatant, and William Drew and Margaret as non-combatants) joined the fight. In total, some 180,000 black men joined the Union Army.

Blacks also supported the Union Army as 'carpenters, chaplains, cooks, guards, laborers, nurses, scouts, spies, steamboat pilots, surgeons, and teamsters'. And black women served, 'as nurses, spies, and scouts'.[1]

For the South, 'Blacks, both free and enslaved, 'were used for manual labor', but there was hostility 'to any efforts' to arm them. However, 'desperate circumstances' meant that the Confederacy 'changed its policy in the last month of the war'.[2] But by this time, it was too late to affect the outcome.

For those Blacks who fought for, or aided the Union forces, the hope was, of course, that if the Union were to be victorious, then slavery would be abolished throughout the United States.

The enslaved were not to be disappointed because, on 22 September 1862, in the second year of the Civil War, US President Abraham Lincoln issued the 'Emancipation Proclamation'. According to the proclamation, on 1 January 1863, all persons held as slaves shall be then, thenceforward, and forever free'.[3]

By nailing his colours to the proverbial mast, Lincoln had not only offered hope to the enslaved, but also provided the strongest motivation to Blacks to fight for the success of the Union forces.

The war ended on 9 April 1865. On 6 December 1865, the 13th Amendment to the American Constitution was ratified, and proclaimed on 18 December 1865. This 'confirmed freedom' for all slaves throughout the USA.[4] It was therefore just before Christmas that the enslaved were finally granted their liberty.

1. Military history of African Americans in the American Civil War, *Wikipedia,* op. cit.
2. Ibid.
3. 'Emancipation Proclamation', *Wikipedia.*
4. Walvin, James, *The Hutchinson Encyclopedia.*

CHAPTER 44

What Became of Ezekiel and Margaret

After the Civil War, William Drew began a new life in Pennsylvania, as will be seen.

After Emancipation (18 December 1865), said Lloyd L. Brown, 'Ezekiel and his sister Margaret, 'returned to be part of the extended family of Benjamin and Sabra'.[1] This is confirmed by the 1870 Census, which reveals that in 1870 all three families were neigbours, living at Williamston, Martin County, North Carolina. (Williamston is about 11 miles to the east of Robersonville.) The details are as follows:

Benjamin Congleton, aged 50, farm labourer; 'inferred spouse' Sabra Congleton, aged 45, 'keeping house'; children Hannah, aged 16; Esther, aged 14; John, aged 12, all farm hands. This indicates that Benjamin and Sabra now had three more children.

Ezekiel Congleton (note, he is now using his father's surname), 'farm hand', aged 30; 'inferred spouse' Gatsy (née Coefield) aged 25, 'keeping house'; 'inferred children': Martha aged 2, and Harriet aged 1. Gatsy would bear Ezekiel a total of thirteen children.

Margaret, aged 25, 'keeping house', father Benjamin Congleton, married to Silas Andrews, aged 35, 'Farm Hand'; daughter Edny, aged 12.

It was also stated that neither Ezekiel nor Margaret could read or write.

A decade later, in 1880 the Census indicates that Benjamin and Ezekiel and their families had relocated to Cross Roads Township, Martin County, 6 miles east of Robersonville. Ezekiel was now using the surname 'Roberson'. It is likely that Margaret and family also relocated to Cross Roads Township.

The 1890 Census for NC was, unfortunately, virtually completely destroyed by fire in 1921.

Brown stated that 'around the turn of the century, Rev. William Robeson took his only daughter, Marian Marguerite [sic Margaret], on a trip from their home in Princeton, New Jersey to Martin County to visit that sister [Margaret] for whom he had given Marian her middle name; and Marian recalled seeing a field of cotton for the first time and having her Aunt Margaret show her how cotton was picked'.[2]

Finally, by 1920, Ezekiel has a home of his own and is employed on his 'own account'. Clearly, he had made good!

1. Brown, Lloyd L., *The Young Paul Robeson: On My Journey Now*, p.140.
2. Brown, Lloyd L., *The Young Paul Robeson: On My Journey Now*, op. cit., p.14.

CHAPTER 45

What Became of Paul's Father, William Drew Robeson?

After the Civil War, when William Drew began a new life in Pennsylvania, he attended a 'Freedmen's School'.[1] 'The Freedmen's Bureau, formally known as the 'Bureau of Refugees, Freedmen and Abandoned Lands', was established in 1865 by Congress to help millions of former black slaves and poor Whites in the South in the aftermath of the Civil War. The Freedmen's Bureau provided food, housing, and medical aid, established schools and offered legal assistance'.[2]

In autumn 1867, William Drew commenced a 'one-year preparatory class' at Lincoln University, near Oxford, Pennsylvania.[3] The university was 'Originally established as The Ashmun Institute', and had 'received its charter from the Commonwealth of Pennsylvania on 29 April 1854, making it the nation's first degree-granting historically Black College and University (HBCU)'.[4]

Said Paul junior, 'During his studies at Lincoln, William Drew met Maria Louisa Bustill, a young Philadelphian teacher, who frequently visited her uncle's house in the nearby town of Lincoln'.[5]

In 1873, Benjamin was awarded the degree Bachelor of Arts, and on 6 June 1876, the degrees of Master of Arts and Bachelor of Sacred Theology.[6] For William Drew, a former slave whose parents could neither read nor write, this was a truly remarkable metamorphosis![7]

On 11 July 1878, William Drew and Maria Louisa were married. Said Paul junior, Maria Louisa 'married the earnest divinity student who excelled in ancient languages'.[8]

William had recently adopted the middle name of 'Drew', said Lloyd L. Brown, 'perhaps from the noted actor John Drew'.[9] This was a reference to US stage actor, John Drew junior (1853-1927), noted for his roles in Shakespearean comedy.

William Drew would have been particularly proud of the fact that several of his wife, Maria Louisa's relatives had been active members of the Underground Railroad.

Subsequently, said Paul, 'Following a brief pastorate in Wilkes-Barre, Pennsylvania [112 miles north-west of Philadelphia] he was called, in 1880, to be pastor of the Witherspoon Street Presbyterian Church in Princeton, New Jersey',[10] in which capacity he served from 1880-1901. Furthermore, two of William Drew's brothers followed him to the city of Princeton: namely, Benjamin junior and John, together with their families.[11]

However, said Betty Moore, a neighbour of the Robesons at Princeton, 'The church itself was run by the white people, and they tell the church what to do. The church was not a black church', though 'we have some black people coming here'.[12]

1. Robeson, Paul, Jr. *The Undiscovered Paul Robeson: An Artist's Journey, 1898-1939*, p.4.
2. Freedmen's Bureau, History.com Editors, online.
3. Robeson, Paul, Jr. *The Undiscovered Paul Robeson: An Artist's Journey, 1898-1939*, op. cit., p.4.
4. Lincoln University: History, online.
5. Robeson, Paul, Jr., *The Undiscovered Paul Robeson: An Artist's Journey, 1898-1939*, op. cit., p.4.
6. Brown, Lloyd L., *The Young Paul Robeson: On My Journey Now*, p.17.
7. US Federal Census, 1880.
8. Robeson, Paul, Jr. *The Undiscovered Paul Robeson: An Artist's Journey, 1898-1939*, op. cit., p.4.
9. Brown, Lloyd L., *The Young Paul Robeson: On My Journey Now*, op. cit., p.17.
10. Robeson, Paul, with Lloyd L. Brown, *Here I Stand*, op. cit., p.6.
11. Brown, Lloyd L., *The Young Paul Robeson: On My Journey Now*, op. cit., p.21.
12. *'Paul Robeson: Here I Stand', PBS American Masters, 1999.

CHAPTER 46

Were Slave Owners Universally Cruel?

There is no doubt that some slave owners were immensely cruel to their defenceless black slaves.[1] But this was not always the case. Eslanda, for example, whose late paternal great-grandmother, Lydia Weston had been a slave, stated that 'The Blacks when in slavery were the most loved and trusted of servants. The flower of white manhood in the South often left their wives, children, and homes to the care of some trusted Negro when he had to be away for any length of time. This confidence and trust were rarely abused. The Blacks were acknowledged as a loyal, faithful, and loving race.'

This being said, Eslanda was under no illusion about the hardships endured by the slaves after liberation. After the Civil War, everything changed, she said. 'The huge plantations of the South required labour on a large scale which had heretofore been slave labour. Many of the original 'southern gentlemen' had been killed or had lost their fortunes in the war, and the new owners were often former overseers or "Poor Whites". All owners naturally, resented paying for labour which had been free only a few years before. If, instead of saying "Yes, suh, thank you, suh", and retiring to his cabin, the now freed black labourer held out his hand for his wage, and perhaps dared to argue about that wage, he was considered impertinent and "uppity" and to have "forgotten his place".'

As a result, 'Many of the freed Negroes began to migrate to the north, and the southern white man, resenting his untilled fields, began to hate the "Northern" Negro.[2]

The family *Bible* that belonged to William Roberson and his wife, Sally (née Wynn), the parents of William Wynn Roberson, George Outlaw Roberson, and Henry Daniel Roberson survives. It was printed and published by Holbrook & Fessenden of Brattleborough, Vermont in 1828. In addition to recording birth and death dates for members of the family, the births of thirteen African American slaves were also recorded.

The *Holy Bible* was a treasured and revered book, which would have been consulted regularly and read aloud perhaps, on a daily basis, but definitely on Sundays. It provided a tangible link to the pioneer ancestors and, of course, to the word of God. So why were details of the family's African American slaves recorded in it? The *Bible* was surely not being used for such a mundane purpose as an inventory for business purposes! No, the conclusion must be that the newborn slaves were regarded both as members of the Roberson family, and also as the children of God.

1. Hermence, Belinda, *My Folks don't want me to Talk about Slavery.*
2. Robeson, Eslanda Goode, *Paul Robeson: Negro,* pp.54-5.

CHAPTER 47

How Paul's Songs Resonated Throughout the World

In respect of his music, said Paul, 'If I can recreate for an audience the great sadness of the Negro slave in 'Sometimes I Feel like a Motherless Child', or if I make them know the strong, gallant convict of the chain gang; make them feel his thirst; understand his naive boasting about his strength; feel the brave gaiety and sadness in 'Water Boy'; if I can explain to them the simple, divine faith of the Negro in 'Weepin' Mary', then I shall increase their knowledge and understanding of my people'.

Chain gang: a group of convicts chained together while working outside the prison.[1]

'They will sense that we are moved by the same emotions, have the same beliefs, the same longings - that we are all human together. That will be something to work for, something' worth doing.'[2]

---

1. Stevenson, A., and Waite, M., *Concise Oxford English Dictionary*.
2. Robeson, Eslanda Goode, *Paul Robeson: Negro*, pp.85-6.

CHAPTER 48

Paul's Final Years: Charlotte Turner Bell

It is Charlotte Turner Bell, a resident of Philadelphia, whom we have to thank for an insightful account of Paul's later years. Charlotte was a piano teacher and a near neighbour of Paul's widowed sister, Marian Forsyth in Philadelphia, Pennsylvania. Marian's husband, William had died in 1959. When Marian invited Charlotte to pay Paul a visit, this resulted in a lasting and fruitful friendship for both of them.[1]

In the summer of 1966, Paul paid a visit to Marian, after which he returned to New York in September to reside with his son, Paul Junior and family.[2] However, in October 1966, he returned to Philadelphia.

4951 Walnut Street, Philadelphia, is a three-storey, semi-detached, gabled house, which Marian's late husband, Dr William Forsythe a medical doctor, had purchased in the late 1950s. William had died in 1959. Paul would reside here with Marian and her daughter, Paulina for the remainder of his days.

Paul's usual routine was as follows, said Charlotte. He 'would get up around noon, take a shower, dress completely with his white shirt and tie' which, 'I suppose he had been accustomed to wearing through the years. After dressing he would go downstairs, sit at the dining room table, and look over the morning paper until the housekeeper served his breakfast. He always enjoyed his meals'.

'Some days Paul preferred to stay in bed and get a good rest.' However, 'once downstairs he would stay for the rest of the day' until 'rather late at night to watch some television programs'. He watched 'most of the college and professional games' of football on television, 'discussing the good and bad points with Pauli [Paul junior] over the phone. He also enjoyed 'musical shows', 'and went to the movies at various times to see 'Guess Who's Coming to Dinner', 'Oklahoma', and also the live musical, 'Hello Dolly'.

'Marian would take him shopping at various seasons of the year for suits, shoes, etc. Since Paul was very tall, (six feet two inches) she took him to a very exclusive store for tall men that sold imported items.'[3]

Occasionally, Paul travelled 'with his sister to her summer home in Pleasantville, New Jersey: a very picturesque seashore town'. Whereupon Paul told Marian 'that walking by the ocean made him feel years younger'.[4]

Charlotte began accompanying Paul privately, on the piano in mid-October 1966, and Paul junior 'brought a great deal of his father's music down from New York. Paul would look through different books and solos, and usually he would decide to sing a number of spirituals that he had sung in concert'.[5]

Paul junior was a true son of his father. It will be remembered that Paul senior's brother, Reeve was christened 'John Bunyan Reeve Robeson'. Paul senior would surely have been aware that John Bunyan was a 17th century Christian writer and Puritan preacher. Perhaps the words of Bunyan's Christian allegory *Pilgrim's Progress* (1684) crossed Paul senior's mind, in respect of his beloved son: 'My sword I give to him that shall succeed me in my pilgrimage …'.

Some of Paul's favourite spirituals, said Charlotte, were 'I've Been Through the Storm, So Long'; 'Witness'; 'Break Bread Together'; 'Ol' Man River'; 'All Through the Night' (in German). and 'Water Boy'. When he sang 'Old Time Religion'; 'Climbing Jacob's Ladder', and 'He's Got the Whole World in His Hands', he would sing them with such feeling. He would sit with his eyes closed while singing and a broad smile on his face. Most of the time he sang sitting by the piano'.[6]

When Paul read Lincoln's Gettysburg Address, said Charlotte, 'I softly played 'The Battle Hymn of the Republic', and he sang it at the end of the reading'.[7]

'Mine eyes have seen the glory of the coming of the Lord;
He is trampling out the vintage where the grapes of wrath are stored;
He hath loosed the fateful lightning of His terrible swift sword:
His truth is marching on.

(Chorus)
Glory, glory, hallelujah!
Glory, glory, hallelujah!
Glory, glory, hallelujah!
His truth is marching on.'

The lyrics were written by US poet, author, and abolitionist, Julia Ward Howe to the tune of 'John Brown's Body'.

'Paul would relax after singing by reading poetry, drama, and by reading aloud for his sister and me the current news from French and

German newspapers. They were his choice foreign languages, even though he spoke many African, Asiatic, and European languages. He would translate the news into English for us.'[8]

Another person who accompanied Paul on the piano was Elizabeth Arnold Michael 'who lived in the same block with her husband, Dr E. Raphael Michael and their two daughters'. Elizabeth 'vocalized' with Paul, recalled her daughter, Vernoca. Also, said Vernoca, her father, Dr Michael, Minister of Wesley AME Zion Church and lecturer and teacher at various colleges and seminars, was Paul's 'spiritual mentor'.[9] Vernoca is now executive director of the Paul Robeson House & Museum in Philadelphia, PA.

Paul's 'faithful sister, Marian and the rest of the family saw to it that he was never lonely. They made provisions so that he never had to go into a nursing home.[10] Paul's lifelong friends in Philadelphia visited him often: taking him for drives through historical Philadelphia to see some of the vast changes which had been made. Close friends from out of town visited him at various times too. He was always happy to see them and Marian would make their visit very pleasant by serving special dinners'.

Among the visitors, said Charlotte, were Lloyd L. Brown; Samuel Rosen, ear specialist, Mount Sinai Hospital, Manhattan; Harry Belafonte; actors and civil rights activists, Ossie Davis and his wife, Ruby Dee; Bishop J. W. Walls, Head of the Second Episcopal District of the AME Zion Church; Bishop J. Clinton Hoggard, Presiding Prelate of the Sixth Episcopal District of the AME Zion Church, and Paul's former accompanist, Laurence Brown.

'Pauli and his wife, Marilyn and his grandchildren, Susan and David, frequently visited him; and also, his late brother, the Reverend Benjamin Robeson's children from New York.'[11]

Charlotte described how she had attended the 'Salute to Paul Robeson', a celebration of Paul's 75th birthday, held at New York's Carnegie Hall. The birthday had occurred on 9 April 1973, but the celebration was held 6 days later, on 15 April. Said she, 'The most moving part of the entire program was when Paul appeared on film on a large screen and his taped message for the birthday celebration was delivered. He said in his message:

'Warmest thanks to all the many friends here and throughout the world who have sent me greetings on my seventy-fifth birthday. Though I have not been able to be active for several years, I want you to know that I am the same Paul, dedicated as ever to the worldwide cause of humanity for freedom, peace, and brotherhood. Though ill health has compelled my retirement, you can be sure that in my heart I go on singing –

> But I keeps laughing
> Instead of crying
> I must keep fighting
> Until I'm dying
> And Ol' Man River
> He just keeps rolling along!'

The above words are from the song 'Ol' Man River', from the 1927 musical, *Show Boat* where the plight of the African Americans is contrasted with the endless, uncaring flow of the Mississippi River. In other words, 'Mississippi' is a metaphor for white supremacy; white indifference; 'Uncle Sam'.

'It was a dramatic moment', said Charlotte, 'and the applause from the audience lasted for almost twenty minutes.'[12] At the celebration, said Charlotte, Paul junior 'paid the finest tribute a son could give to his father':

'The most important thing my father has done for me does not derive from his great fame, or even from his magnificent intellect. What means most to me is the fact that from as far back as I can remember he has, in his own special way, helped me to be a better human being. One cannot thank a father for such a gift - one can only treasure it and carry it always in one's heart.'

Paul delivered his final public address to the Actors' Equity Association, NYC, on 1 June 1974: 'To all the young people, black and white, who are so passionately concerned with making a better world, and to all the old timers who have been involved in that struggle, I say: Right On!'[13]

It was on 28 December 1975 that Paul was admitted to Philadelphia's Presbyterian Medical Center, having suffered a stroke. Said Paul junior, the FBI continued its surveillance of Paul, 'even when he was in hospital, including during his last illness'.[14] Paul died on 23 January 1976 at the age of 77. As had been the case with Eslanda, he was buried at Ferncliffe Cemetery, Hartsdale, Westchester County, New York. Marian herself died on 17 February 1977.

When news of Paul's death was announced, said Charlotte, 'immediately all of the radio stations in Philadelphia began to play Paul's records as a tribute to his memory, presenting highlights of his life from his youth to his last days in public life. Several of his dramatic records also were played: the "Monologue from *Othello*", and the "Monologue from Boris Godunov" [opera by Mussorgsky]. Clips from various movies he made were shown for several nights on television': for example, *Emperor Jones*; *Proud Valley*; *Saunders of the River*; and *Freedom*'.

'Radio and television stations continued to pay tribute to Paul at various times each day until his funeral, which was held in New York City on 27 January 1976 at Mother AME Zion Church where his brother, the late Reverend Benjamin Robeson had pastored for twenty-seven years.' The church, which had a capacity of 2,500, 'was packed and just as many rain-drenched people stood outside. The Cathedral Choir and audience sang Paul's favourite spiritual at the beginning of the service, 'We Are Climbing Jacob's Ladder'.[15]

Paul junior paid this tribute. 'I cannot speak today of the full measure of the family's personal grief and overflowing sense of loss.' 'To all of us', he said, 'he gave by example a set of standards to guide our lives, each of us in our own way. But I speak today not only because I loved him as a father; I loved him as a friend and as a great and gentle warrior with whom I worked and fought, side by side.'[16]

1. Bell, Charlotte Turner, *Paul Robeson's Last Day in Philadelphia*, p.1.
2. Ibid, p.3
3. Ibid, pp.4-5.
4. Ibid, pp.2-3.
5. Ibid, p.6.
6. Ibid, p.6.
7. Ibid, pp.7-8.
8. Ibid, p.8.
9. 'History of Paul Robeson House', Paul Robeson House & Museum.
10. Bell, Charlotte Turner, *Paul Robeson's Last Day in Philadelphia*, op. cit., p.11.
11. Ibid, p.11.
12. Ibid, pp.12-13.
13. Foner, Philip S., *Paul Robeson Speaks*, p.483.
14. *'Paul Robeson: Here I Stand', PBS American Masters, 1999.
15. Bell, Charlotte Turner, *Paul Robeson's Last Day in Philadelphia*, op. cit., pp.17-18.
16. Ibid, pp.25-6.

CHAPTER 49

Paul's Religious Beliefs

Although Paul seldom discussed his religious beliefs, in an interview which he gave in 1960 for Australian television he referred to 'our church'. 'We are very religious people', he said. He was also proud of the fact that his late father, William Drew had been a pastor and so currently, was his brother, Benjamin. In fact, his strong religious faith underpinned his whole being.

Subsequently, referring to the Mother AME Zion Church in NYC, where Benjamin had been pastor from 1936 to 1963, Bishop J. Clinton Hoggard stated that 'when Paul was in the United States he worshipped regularly in this sanctuary as a modest, humble, unobtrusive member'.[1] And during Paul's later years in Philadelphia, said Bishop Hoggard, 'my brother', the Reverend Aaron Hoggard, 'a pastor' at the local Saint James AME Zion Church, 'would visit Paul, have prayer with him, take him for automobile rides, and find great happiness in his presence'.[2]

Clearly, Paul had deep religious convictions, and it is doubtful whether anyone could have sung Negro Spirituals with such power and feeling without such convictions.

1. Bell, Charlotte Turner, *Paul Robeson's Last Day in Philadelphia*, p.23.
2. Ibid, p.25.

CHAPTER 50

Epilogue

No actor, black or white, before, or since, has brought to the stage or screen, such a combination of magnificent physical presence, supreme intelligence, a wondrous speaking and singing voice, combined with such genuine compassion, humanity, and dignity as Paul Robeson. Nor has anyone possessed finer linguistic, oratorial, and debating skills: qualities of supreme importance when it came to the movement for civil rights, for which he worked unstintingly, all his adult life.

Said Anthony ('Tony') Wedgwood Benn, UK politician, writer, and diarist, it was Paul's 'awareness of prejudice when he was young that really gave him an authenticity, which you would not have got from reading Karl Marx when you were a kid and deciding if you were a communist'.[1]

Said Susan Robeson, 'Paul was able to live and see the world catch up with him, and validate the very things that he had been persecuted for and hounded for'.[2]

Said Harry Belafonte, if Paul 'were to come back at this very moment, he would assess and evaluate where the losses are and the victories have been, and how to regroup, and how to get on, because the enemy is still there'.[3]

Perhaps the most eloquent tribute to Paul was the one paid to him at his funeral by his dear friend, Lloyd L. Brown: 'The tallest tree in our forest has fallen. Something uniquely wonderful has departed from the Earth. Robeson was a modern-day Black American with the manifold talents of a Renaissance man.'[4]

Who else, in the 20th century or indeed, in any other century, has distinguished himself or herself in so many different spheres of life: debate; oratory; musicianship; singing; athletics; sport; film and theatre acting; linguistics? Robeson's voice is, arguably, the finest male bass baritone in history, bar none, and those who hear it may imagine that they are picking cotton in the USA's 'Deep South'; standing on the banks of the Mississippi River – 'Ol' Man River'; watching Paul as he cuddles his

'Curly Headed Baby' in his arms; or being conveyed to heaven in a 'Sweet Chariot'!

But above all, Paul was a source of inspiration to the poor, underprivileged and downtrodden the world over, no matter what their colour or creed. He was Moses, Joshua, David (though in physique he was more like Goliath!) all rolled into one. For him, the 'Promised Land' was achievable for everybody. That, is his greatest and enduring legacy!

1. *'Paul Robeson: Here I Stand', PBS American Masters, 1999.
2. Ibid.
3. Ibid.
4. Brown, Lloyd L., *The Young Paul Robeson: On My Journey Now*, p.29

APPENDICES

Appendix 1: Some of Paul's Lifetime Awards and Recognitions

In June 1919, Paul won the Ann Van Nest Bussing Prize in Extempore Speaking

In October 1949 in the Soviet Union, a newly discovered peak in Kazakstan was named 'Mount Robeson' in Paul's honour.

On 23 September 1952, Paul was presented with the 1952 Stalin Peace Prize by Dr W. E. B. Du Bois at a ceremony at New York's Theresa Hotel.[1] The prize had originally been created as the International Stalin Prize for Strengthening Peace Among Peoples on 21 December 1949. This was by executive order of the Praesidium of the Supreme Soviet in honour of Joseph Stalin's 70th birthday (the date of which was, in fact, 21 December 1948).

On 29 January 1953 the National Church of Nigeria named Paul, 'Champion of African Freedom', an award granted for 'selfless service to Africa'.[2]

On 14 September 1954, Paul was made an honorary professor by the Moscow State Conservatory of Music.[3]

In January 1963, the Paul Robeson Choir was established in Berlin, German Democratic Republic.[4]

On 2 April 1969, the 'Paul Robeson Music and Arts Lounge' was 'dedicated in a new student center at Rutgers University'.[5]

On 15 November 1970, at a ceremony at the New York Hilton Hotel, Paul was presented with the Zhitlovsky Award by the Zhitlovsky Foundation for Jewish education.[6]

Chaim Zhitlovsky (1865-1943): Jewish communist and political thinker.

On 16 April 1973, a 'Salute to Paul Robeson Exhibition' opened at Gallery 1199 of the Drug and Hospital Workers' Union, NYC.[7]

On 3 June 1973, Paul was awarded Doctor of Law by Lincoln University, Pennsylvania.[8]

In June 1974, in his last public statement, Paul became the first recipient of an award named for him by the Actors' Equity Association.[9]

1. Foner, Philip S., *Paul Robeson Speaks*, op. cit., p.41.
2. Ibid, p.41.
3. Ibid, p.43.
4. Ibid, p.44.
5. Ibid, p.45.
6. Ibid, p.45.
7. Ibid, p.45.
8. Ibid, p.46.
9. Ibid, p.46.

Appendix 2: The Manilla

In West Africa in the time of slavery, the local currency was the manilla. The size and shape of a horseshoe, manillas were manufactured on an industrial scale in Britain. The 'King manilla' was highly decorated, and more valuable than the standard manilla. One manilla might be exchanged for ten slaves. Therefore, the lives of each of Benjamin and Sabra's forebears, when they were traded in West Africa, were each valued at one-tenth of a manilla.

Appendix 3: George Washington's Personal Standard

Cousins, Fannie B. Lovell and Ellen Lovell Crosby, descendants of Betty Washington Lewis (George Washington's sister), donated this silk flag to Reverend W. Herbert Burk's museum of American history at Valley Forge in 1910.

W. Herbert Burk (1867-1933) was an Episcopal priest and founding vicar of the Washington Memorial Chapel in the Valley Forge National Historical Park.

Two of Lewis's sons served as private secretaries for Washington, and a third served as an officer in Washington's 'Life Guard' during the Revolutionary War. According to family tradition, this flag marked the presence of General Washington throughout much of the war. Also known as a standard due to its modest size, it is believed to be the earliest surviving 13-star American flag. The Reverend Burk's 'Valley Forge Historical Society', the predecessor organization of the 'Museum of the American Revolution', served as the long-time steward of Washington's standard. Museum of the American Revolution, Philadelphia, USA.

Appendix 4: Evolution of the 'Stars and Stripes'

'Between 1777 and 1960, Congress passed several acts that changed the shape, design and arrangement of the flag and allowed for additional stars and stripes to be added to reflect the admission of each new state to the Union:

Act of 13 January 1794: provided for 15 stripes and 15 stars after May 1795.
Act of 4 April 1818: provided for 13 stripes and one star for each state, to be added to the flag on the 4th of July following the admission of each new state, signed by President Monroe.
Executive Order of President Taft, 24 June 1912: established proportions of the flag and provided for arrangement of the stars in six horizontal rows of eight each, a single point of each star to be upward.
Executive Order of President Eisenhower, 3 January 1959: provided for the arrangement of the stars in seven rows of seven stars each, staggered horizontally and vertically.
Executive Order of President Eisenhower, 21 August 1959: provided for the arrangement of the stars in nine rows of stars staggered horizontally and eleven rows of stars staggered vertically.'[1]

Appendix 4: Evolution of the 'Stars and Stripes'

1. 'Brand New Flag', Flag History, online.

Appendix 5: The Paul Robeson House & Museum, 4951 Walnut Street, Philadelphia, PA.

'After Paul died in 1976, and Marian a year later, the house was left to Paulina. 'It had been vacant for more than 12 years when the West Philadelphia Cultural Alliance (WPCA) bought it in 1994. So, the alliance, under the direction of Frances P. Aulston, the driving force behind the house, went about restoring it as a legacy to Robeson.' Frances (1940-2015) was an educator, a cultural historian, and President and CEO of The Paul Robeson House and of the WPCA.

'In 2000, the house became an Official Project of Save America's Treasures, and is listed on the National Register for Historic Places.'[1]

Appendix 5: The Paul Robeson House & Museum, 4951 Walnut Street, Philadelphia, PA.

1. 'History of Paul Robeson House', Paul Robeson House & Museum.

Appendix 6: A Church in Dorset and its Connection with the 'Stars and Stripes'.

Nestling in the rolling hills of Purbeck in Dorset, 20 miles or so from my home in Poole, lies the tiny hamlet of Steeple, whose 13th century church of St Michael & All Angels, (which, ironically, has no steeple!) contains clues as to why the flag of the US is designed the way it is.

The observant visitor will notice in the main porch, a stone-carved armorial escutcheon (shield), and a similar one over the east doorway of the north transept. They depict the arms of Edmund Lawrence of nearby Creech Grange (a descendant of Edward and Agnes Lawrence), together with his initials and the date '1616', quartered with those of heiress, Agnes de Wessington (an alternative spelling of Washington).

Armorial: relating to heraldry of heraldic devices

Quarter: in heraldry, each of four or more (four in this case) roughly equal divisions of a shield.[1]

The same coat of arms is represented on several bosses on the barrel roof of the nave.

The coat of arms of 'Washington' dates back to the 12th century when the family took possession of Washington Old Hall in County Durham.

The marriage of Edmund and Agnes, both residents of the Duchy of Lancaster in north-west England, took place 1390. Their descendants relocated to Steeple in 1540, while John Washington, 'a member of a junior branch of Agnes's family', emigrated to Virginia. In Virginia, the Washingtons prospered and John's great-grandson, George, became the 1st President of the US.

On the escutcheon which bears the arms is a 'Crusader Cross' which quarters the mullets and bars of the Washington coat of arms.

Mullets: stars, in this case three.
Bars: horizontal bands, in this case two.

The ceiling bosses take the form of more escutcheons, the stars and bands ('stripes') of the Lawrence/Washington coats of arms being painted in scarlet on a white background. The Lawrence/Washington coat of arms evolved with minor alterations over the years, the designs on the aforementioned shields being based on that of the coat of arms granted to George Washington's great-grandfather x3, Lawrence Washington of Sulgrave Manor, Northamptonshire in 1592.

This coat of arms was used privately by the president in his home at Mount Vernon, for example on his signet ring, on his gold fob seal, and on his ink stand.[2]

The 'Stars and Stripes' flag, or 'Old Glory'

During the Revolutionary War, George Washington's Commander-in-Chief's personal standard flew over his headquarters, wherever that happened to be at the time. The flag features 13 white stars, representing the 13 colonies, on a blue background.[3]

On 14 June 1777, 'to establish an official flag for the new nation, the Continental Congress passed the first Flag Act: "Resolved, that the flag of the United States be made of thirteen stripes, alternate red and white; that the union be thirteen stars, white in a blue field, representing a new Constellation"'.[4]

Clearly therefore, Washington's headquarters flag was copied for the 'Stars' element of the 'Stars and Stripes' flag (a difference being that on Washington's standard, the stars were 6-pointed, whereas on the Stars and Stripes flag, the stars are 5-pointed).

As regards the red horizontal 'Stripes', it seems likely that the idea for these derived from Washington's own coat of arms.

'Today the American flag consists of thirteen horizontal stripes, 7 red, alternating with 6 white. The stripes represent the original 13 colonies, and the stars represent the 50 states of the Union.'[5]

The flag of Washington, DC

The design of the flag of the capital city of the USA is identical in design to the coat of arms granted to George Washington's - great-grandfather x2, Lawrence Washington in 1592. 'In 1938, the flag was selected by a commission created by Act of Congress with the help of the Commission of Fine Arts. Today, it can be seen all around the city on DC Government property, flying in front of homes, in logos of local businesses and on some local residents' bodies as tattoos. It is also flown proudly on Flag Day [14 June].'[6]

In July 1977, the Rector of St. Michael & All Angels, Steeple, received a letter from Walter E. Washington, Mayor of the District of Columbia:

'Dear Rector,

We recently learned through Mr George Honebon of Poole, that the Church of St Michael & All Angels has an historic relationship with the family of George Washington, in whose honor our Nation's Capital is named.

It was particularly interesting to see drawings of the stone armorial tablet depicting the Washington arms quartered with those of Lawrence. Because they are shown in our flag, the Washington arms are a very familiar sight in the District of Columbia.

Thinking that your parish might appreciate having some token of our mutual heritage, I have asked Mr Honebon to carry with him on his return to England, this letter and the Flag of Washington, District of Columbia.

I know the citizens of our city join with me in this expression of friendship and best wishes to you and all the people of the community of Steeple, Dorset.

With warm personal regards.

Sincerely ... '

On 21 September 1942, Paul had led the workers of Moore Shipyard, Oakland, CA, in the singing of the 'Star Spangled Banner' during their lunch hour.

The 'Star-Spangled Banner': the national anthem of the US, which was clearly composed with the national flag, the 'Stars and Stripes' in mind. The lyrics, by Maryland lawyer and amateur poet, Francis Scott Key are set to the tune of a popular song by British composer, church organist, and musicologist, John Stafford Smith.

Afterwards, referring to the current war with Germany, Paul told them, 'This is a serious job, winning this war against fascists. We have to be together'. Paul himself had been a shipyard worker during the First World War.

> 'O say can you see, by the dawn's early light,
> What so proudly we hailed at the twilight's last gleaming,
> Whose broad stripes and bright stars through the perilous fight,
> O'er the ramparts we watched, were so gallantly streaming?
> And the rocket's red glare, the bombs bursting in air,
> Gave proof through the night that our flag was still there;
> O say does that star-spangled banner yet wave
> O'er the land of the free and the home of the brave?'

1. Stevenson, A., and Waite, M., *Concise Oxford English Dictionary*.
2. *Wikipedia*.
3. See Appendix 3: George Washington's Personal Standard.
4. 'Brand New Flag', Flag History, online.
5. Ibid.
6. 'The Flag of Washington, DC', *Wikipedia*.

Appendix 7: Tammy Roberson James, Robersonville, North Carolina, USA, 6 January 2021

Said Tammy Roberson James, 'I started out in the world in a little bitty town called Robersonville. It happened that my maiden name would be Roberson and I would live on Roberson Street too. As I got older and ventured further out to neighboring cities, people would joke about my name that I shared with my town. "So, did they name the town after you or are you named after the town?" is the sort of question I would hear followed with a chuckle. This would cause my curiosity to peak and so I started digging. I learned that my family laid the groundwork for the town I call home. The very street I started on was the street that was home to my great-great grandfather George Outlaw Roberson's many businesses. I would also learn that in his time of existence there was a dark period of civil war and slavery. I continued to gather more history about my ancestors and still remain hungry to learn more. Recently, I've learned that a runaway slave William Drew Robeson was linked to my family has a famous descendant. I am intrigued and eager to learn more about Paul Robeson and how he became successful and world renowned despite the many difficult hardships his family endured for so many years. It reminds me that no matter the circumstances, you can have much success in life. I especially thank Dr. Andrew Norman for helping me to learn more.'

Appendix 8: Stephen A. Bess, Rockville, Maryland, USA, 9 January 2021

Said Stephen A. Bess, 'I do not remember the first time that I heard Paul Robeson's name, but I do remember that he became an especially important part of my life after I returned home from serving in the Navy in the spring of 1988. The following year, I enrolled as a freshman at Savannah State College (now Savannah State University) in Savannah, Georgia. In the classroom, I would talk about Paul Robeson to anyone who was willing to listen, and I would write about him in my journals in freshman composition. My professors seemed impressed that I knew of him and even more impressed that I am related. Many of the freshman students had never heard of Paul Robeson because he nor many other noteworthy Black Americans, outside of the Reverend Martin Luther King Jr. or Harriet Tubman, were mentioned in high school history class. I am a descendant of Paul Robeson's uncle, Ezekiel Roberson.

Overtime, I have come to recognize the rarity and importance of that family history that spreads like seed among the Dogwood and Pecan trees across the Cross Roads Township of Martin County and the town Robersonville, North Carolina. I have come to learn that very few Black Americans are acquainted with or can speak of their history and heritage with such certainty. It is a blessing.

I remember the summers traveling "home" down Interstate 95 South to visit my grandparents, Tom and Eunice Roberson Best. Once the car exited Interstate 95 and turned onto North Carolina Highway 125/903, it seemed like I was transported into another place and time. I always enjoyed looking out the window. I loved to watch the endless acres of land and trees that painted the landscape. I remember seeing the farm animals and the occasional Black farm worker and resident who would wave hello to us on that long stretch of highway. As a boy, waving to strangers confused me. Where I was from in Washington, D.C., it was not customary to wave at strangers; however, as I matured, whenever I would see the waving hands, it meant that I was closer to home; so, their waving hands later added to my anticipation. Now, I can appreciate the waves and smiles as something precious because the waving would recede with time. Now, it seems more like they were more waving "goodbye" than "hello" because no one waves much anymore on those back roads that I continue to travel going home. It was a blessing.

Nevertheless, the history remains along those back roads. When I last spoke in person to the late Paul Robeson Jr. at a speaking engagement in Maryland, he informed me that neither he nor his father had ever traveled to Eastern North Carolina to meet their paternal side of the family. Even so, I felt that it carried a special place in their hearts because they would both speak about it with an affection in their speeches and writing. This is the reason I became so excited when I learned of Dr. Andrew Norman's biography. Dr. Norman not only explores the life and legacy of the late and great Paul Robeson, but he also turns off the main road and travels the back roads that leads to the Cross Roads Township in Martin County. He explores and dissects the past in such a way that it seems more like a personal gift than a book. I am grateful for the research and work that Dr. Norman has done to connect all of us to an even more unfamiliar part of Paul Robeson's history. It is my hope that knowing more about the past that continues to surround us will do more to connect us than divide us. That would truly be a blessing.'

Bibliography

Bell, Charlotte Turner, *Paul Robeson's Last Day in Philadelphia*, (Dorrance, Bryn Mawr, Pennsylvania, PA, 1986).

Brown, Lloyd L., *The Young Paul Robeson: On My Journey Now*, (Westfield Press, Boulder, Colorado, USA, 1997).

Butchok, Thomas R., *Martin Architectural Heritage: The Historic Structures of a Rural North Carolina County*, (Martin County Historical Society, Williamston, NC, 1998).

Cron, Frederick H. and Fred W. Harrison, 'In Loving Remembrance of Sabra Robeson' (*North Carolina Genealogical Society Journal*, Volume 46, Number 2, Apr-May-Jun 2020).

Dewey, Philip, 'The Story of Paul Robeson and the Unbreakable Bond he formed with the Miners of Wales', (WalesOnline, 14 April 2019).

Duberman, Martin Bauml, *Paul Robeson*, (Pan Books, London, 1991).

Foner, Philip S., *Paul Robeson Speaks*, (Quartet Books, London, Melbourne, New York, 1978).

Gilchrist, Peter S., 'North Carolina', *Britannica*, 25 September 2020.

Hermence, Belinda, *My Folks don't want me to Talk about Slavery*, (John F. Blair, Winston-Salem, North Carolina, 2001).

Hughes, Jean Nelson (editor), *Martin County Heritage*, (The Martin County Historical Society, Williamston, North Carolina, 1980).

Nicolay, John G. and John Hay, *Complete Works of Abraham Lincoln*, (Harrogate, TN, Lincoln Memorial University, 1894).

Robersonville Centenniel Book, (The Enterprise Publishing Co., Williamston, North Carolina, 1972).

Robeson, Eslanda Goode, *African Journey*, (Victor Gollancz, London, 1946).
Robeson, Eslanda Goode, *Paul Robeson: Negro*, (Victor Gollancz, London, 1930).

Robeson, Paul, with Lloyd L. Brown, *Here I Stand*, (Beacon Press, Boston, 1958).

Robeson, Paul, Jr., *The Undiscovered Paul Robeson: An Artist's Journey, 1898-1939*, (John Wiley, New York, 2001).

Robinson, Jackie, *I Never Had It Made*, (G.P. Putnam's Sons, New York, 1972).

Silber, Irwin (editor), *The Second People's Song Book* (New York, 1953).

Sparrow, Jeff, 'How Paul Robeson found his Political Voice in the Welsh valleys', (*The Observer*, Biography Books online, 2 July 2017).

Stevenson, A., and Waite, M., *Concise Oxford English Dictionary*, (New York, Oxford University Press, 2011).

Walvin, James, *The Hutchinson Encyclopedia*, (Helicon, London, 1999).

Ware, Charles Crossfield, *North Carolina Disciples of Christ*, (Christian Board of Publication, St Louis, Missouri, 1927).

Ware, Charles Crossfield (editor), *Tar Heel Disciples, 1841-1852*, (New Bern, North Carolina, 1942).

*Film Documentaries:

*'Paul Robeson: Here I Stand' (PBS American Masters, 1999).

Index

Ackerman, William A. 34
African Journey 69, 86-87
All God's Chillun Got Wings 48-49, 63
American Civil War. 17, 38, 126, 128-129, 133, 135, 137, 139
American Revolutionary War 17, 24, 34, 152, 154
Amherst College, Amherst, Massachusetts 96
Andrews, Drewpina (see Roberson)
Andrews, Edny 135
Andrews, Margaret (née Congleton) 63
Andrews, Silas 135
Arens, Richard 90, 92-96
Armitage, Teresa 54-56
Atlanta History Center, Atlanta, Georgia. 17
Bagg, Miss 28
Baker, Nancy Ann (see Congleton)
Baltimore, Maryland 126
Bandung Conference 92
Banjo 65
Baynton, Sarah Ann (see Morrey)
Beasley, Ann (see Morrey)
Beaufort County, NC. 114
Belafonte, Harry 63, 75, 144, 148
Bell, Charlotte Turner 142-145
Bengal, Ben 65
Benn, Anthony ('Tony') Neil Wedgwood 64, 148
Benwell, Jane ('Nan') 10
Beneš, Edvard 81
Bess, Stephen A. 122,
Bevan, Aneurin 101
Big Fella 65
Borderline 62
Boston, Massachusetts 31, 53-54
Bowser, David Bustill 17
Brown, Lawrence ('Larry') Benjamin 43, 49-50, 53, 62, 77, 108
Brown, Lloyd Louis 30-31, 48, 62, 108, 124, 129, 135, 137, 144, 148

Bumpus bookshop, 350 Oxford Street, London 59
Bunyan, John 143
Bustill, Cyrus 16-17
Bustill, Gertrude Emily Hicks (see Mossell)
Bustill, Joseph Casey 17
Bustill, Maria Louisa (see Robeson)
Bustill, Maria Louisa (see Robeson)
Bustill, Samuel 16
Cambridge University Socialist Club. 63
Camp, Walter 37, 98
Campbell, Mrs Patrick 43
Cape Town 69
Cardozo, Eslanda Elbert (see Goode)
Cardozo, Lydia (née Weston) 139
Carolina Township, Pitt County, NC 120
Cline, Frances Elizabeth (see Robeson)
Coefield, Gatsey P. (see Roberson)
Cohen, Sarah (see Cardozo)
Cohn, Roy M. 86-88
College Football and All-American 80, 98
Columbia University's Law School, New York City 14, 42-46
Condon, R. L. 43
Congleton, Benjamin (see Benjamin Congleton Robeson)
Congleton, Ezekiel (see Robeson)
Congleton, Hannah 114, 135
Congleton, James R. 116, 120-121
Congleton, Margaret (see Andrews)
Congleton, Temperance Elizabeth, née Gurganus 116, 120-121
Congleton, 'Elder' Henry 120
Continental Congress 84
Cross Roads Township, Martin County, NC 63, 115, 127, 135
Dadoo, Yusuf M. 93
Daily Worker 93
Dandridge, Martha (see Washington)
Daniel, Cynthia Caroline (née Roberson) 127
Daniel, Lanier 127
Davies, Benjamin J. 108
Davis, Benjamin Jefferson junior 95

Davis, Ossie 144
Declaration of Independence 74
Dee, Ruby 144
Dewey, Philip 100
Disciples of Christ 120
Douglas, Frederick 94
Douglas, James 61
Du Bois, William Edward Burghardt 108
Duberman, Martin B. 107
Dulles, John Foster 103
Dunbar, Paul L. 50
Dvořák, Antonín 104
Eastland, James O. 93
Ebbw Vale, South Wales 11, 98, 102
Edinburgh, Scotland, 82
Edwards, Martha 100
Eisenstein, Sergei 63
Elium, Mary Drusilla (see Roberson)
Emancipation Proclamation 133
Emperor Jones, The 48-50, 62-63, 74, 146
Faubus, Orval 98
Feffer, Itzik 82
Foner, Henry 75
Forsythe, Marian Margaret (née Robeson) 142
Forsythe, William Alexander 142
Franco, Francisco 66-67, 94
Freedomways 108
Friedman, Milton 90
Gardiner, Eunice 72
Gardiner, Grace (see Bustill)
German Democratic Republic 98-99, 108
Gettysburg Address 66, 143
Gandhi, Indira 98
Glee Club 28
Goham, Adline (see Congleton)
Goode, Eslanda ('Essie') Cardozo (see Robeson)
Goode, Eslanda Elbert (née Cardozo) 46
Goode, John Jacob 46

Greenberg, Marilyn Paula (see Robeson)
Greenwich Village Theatre, NYC. 49
Grice, Zibe 114
Gurganus, Temperance Elizabeth (see Congleton)
Gurganus, [Willie] 121
Hagen, Uta 75
Haggard, H. Rider 65
Hairy Ape, The 63
Hamilton, NC 126
Harlem, New York 32, 42-44, 48, 50, 74-75, 101, 108
Hayes, Alfred 76
Hayes, Roland 43
Here I Stand 99, 112, 125
Hicks, Elizabeth W. (see Bustill)
Hill, Joe (born Joel Emmanuel Hägglund) 76, 79, 82
Hoggard, J. Clinton 144, 147
Holden, William 129
Horáková, Milada 105
House Un-American Activities Committee (HUAC) 14, 77, 80-81, 86-91, 93, 96
Howard University College of Medicine, Washington DC 31, 46
Howe, Julia Ward 143
Howell, Catherine Romena (see Cardozo)
International Brigade 66-67
Jackson, Yolanda 63
James, Tammy Roberson 127
Janáček, Leoš 104
Jenkins, Susan Caroline (see Roberson)
Jergan, Max 65
Jericho 65
'Jim Crow' 24-25, 28
John Henry 74
Johnson, J. Rosamond 50
'Jumping the broom' 114
Kearney, Bernard William 93-94
Keel, Anna 115
Keel, Samuel Taylor, Josiah 121
Kennedy, John Fitzgerald 73

Kent, Rockwell 103
Kenyatta, Jomo 63
Khrushchev, Nikita 99, 107
King Solomon's Mines 65
*Komsomolskaia 83
Pravda* 83, 99
Korean War 84
Ku Klux Klan 48, 83
Lamont, Corliss 84
Laurel Music Series 54
Law, Oliver 66
Leggett, John 121
Leonard, Gertrude Helen (see Holloway)
Lewis, David Levening 64
Lincoln University, Oxford, Pennsylvania 30-31, 34, 137
Lincoln, Abraham 17, 66, 128, 133
Little Rock, Arkansas 98
London School of Oriental Languages 63
Louverture, Toussaint 34, 65
Margaret 122-123, 126, 128-129, 131-133, 135-136
Matthews, Bunita S. 88
McCarthy, Joseph Raymond 86-87, 90
McKay, Claude 65
McKie, Ronald 72
Michael, E. Raphael 144
Michael, Elizabeth Arnold 144
Michael, Vernoca 144
Middlesex County, New Jersey 34
Moore, Betty 138
Morrey, Elizabeth (see Bustill)
Morrey, Humphrey 16
Mother AME Zion Church, Harlem, New York City 27, 32, 73-74, 108, 144, 146-147
New Bern, Battle of 129
New Bern, Craven County, NC 128-129
New Jersey 24, 31, 42
New York-Presbyterian Hospital, New York City 46, 54
Nichols, Ruby Jean (see Robeson)

Nixon, Richard Milhous 73, 77
Nkrumah, Kwame 63
Norman, Christopher Arthur 10
Norman, Jane (see Savery)
Norman, Jean 10
Oak Grove Primitive Baptist Church, Perkins Township, Pitt County, NC 120
Othello 14, 28, 59-60, 62, 75, 104, 125, 145
Othello Recording Corporation 85
O'Neill, Eugene 48-49, 62-63
Painter, Will 101
Panyushkin, Alexander S. 84
Parthenia 28 16
Paul Robeson House & Museum, 4951 Walnut Street, Philadelphia, PA. 144
Paul Robeson, Negro 16-17, 61-62, 112
Peekskill Riots 83
Peekskill, Westchester County, New York State 80, 83-84
Penn, William 16
People's Republic of China 86
Peter, Paul 64
Philadelphia, Pennsylvania 16-17, 32, 126, 137, 142, 144-145, 147
Phillips, Wendell 34
Pickett, George 128
Pilgrim's Progress 143
Plant in the Sun 65
Port Elizabeth, Cape Province 69
Princeton University, Princeton, New Jersey 25, 37
Princeton, New Jersey 15, 24-27, 30, 135, 138
Proschowsky, Frantz 55
Proud Valley 14, 66, 101, 146
Pushkin, Alexander 82
Quakers 77, 131
Rhondda Valley, South Wales 100-101
Roanoke River 126
Roberson, Cynthia Caroline (see Daniel)
Roberson, Drewpina (née Andrews) 126-127
Roberson, Gatsy P. (née Coefield) 135

Roberson, George Outlaw 125-126, 139
Roberson, Henry 120, 127
Roberson, Henry Daniel 139
Roberson, Joseph L. 129
Roberson, Paul 125
Roberson, Sally Rebecca (née Wynn) 126, 139
Roberson, William Wynn 139
Robersonville, North Carolina 112, 115, 117-128, 135, 137
Robeson, Reverend Benjamin Congleton 74, 108, 144, 146
Robeson, Eslanda Cardozo (née Goode) 16-18, 21-22, 29, 35-37, 42-44, 46, 48-51, 53-63, 65-66, 69-71, 76, 81, 84, 86-89, 107-108, 112, 121-123, 139, 145
Robeson, Ezekiel Congleton 45, 110, 112, 122, 126, 128-129, 131-133, 135-136
Robeson, Frances Elizabeth (née Cline) 32
Robeson, Gatsey (née Coefield) 135
Robeson, John Bunyan Reeve 15, 31, 143
Robeson, Maria Louisa (née Bustill) 13, 15-16, 21, 137
Robeson, Marian Margaret (see Forsythe)
Robeson, Marilyn Paula (née Greenberg) 83
Robeson, Narcissa (née Whitfield) 129
Robeson, Paul Leroy Bustill (Paul junior) 51
Robeson, Ruby Jean (née Nichols) 32
Robeson, Susan 107, 144, 148
Robeson, Vernon 129
Robeson, Reverend William Drew 13, 15-16, 19, 21-23, 28, 32, 35, 57, 96, 110, 112, 122-123, 125-129, 131-133, 135, 137, 147
Robeson, William ('Bill') Drew junior 24-25, 27, 30-31, 34, 50
Robinson, Earl 74, 76-77
Robinson, Emily (see Bustill)
Robson, Flora 63
Roosevelt, Franklin Delano 77, 80
Rosen, Samuel 144
Ross, John L. 121
Rutgers College, New Brunswick, New Jersey 13-14, 34, 36-39, 42, 48, 96
Rutgers University, New Bruswick, New Jersey 37, 48, 93, 108
Rutgers, Henry 34

Sanders of the River 64
Savery, Jane (née Norman) 10
Scherer, Gordon H. 90, 94
Schine, G. David 87
Scott, Hazel 74
Senate Permanent Subcommittee on Investigations of the Committee on Government Operations 86, 89
Senate Permanent Subcommittee on Investigations of the Committee on Government Operations
Shakespeare, William 14, 62, 75, 104
Shaw, George Bernard 62
Shostakovich, Dmitri 103
Show Boat 14, 61, 64, 100
Silvermaster, Nathan Gregory 90
Simon the Cyrenian 43
Sklar, George 64
Škvorecký, Josef 105
Society of Friends (see Quakers)
Solzhenitsyn, Aleksandr 95
Somerville High School, Somerville, New Jersey 28, 30, 34
Song of Freedom 65
Spanish Civil War 65-66
St Luke's AME Zion Church, Downer Street, Westfield, New Jersey. 27
Stalin, Joseph Vissarionovich 83, 95
Stevedore 64
Story of the Only Successful Slave Revolt, The 65
Stotesbury, Louis William 48
Sukarno 91-92
Symington, Stuart 87-88
Taboo 43
Tales of Manhattan 75
Taylor, Clyde 65
The Proud Valley 14, 101, 146
The Undiscovered Paul Robeson 17, 112
The Young Paul Robeson: On My Journey Now 125
Time magazine 83
Todd, Mary (see Lincoln)

Torrence, Frederic Ridgley 43
Touche, John La 74
Trenton, New Jersey 21, 24, 30
Treorchy Male Voice Choir 102
Truman, Harry F. 75, 77
Tubman, Harriet 94, 131
Uganda 69
Underground Railroad 17, 131-132, 137
Union of South Africa 69
Unite Auto Worker (UAW): 'International Union, United Automobile, 75
University of Pennsylvania Medical School, Philadelphia, Pennsylvania 30
Vaughan, David 103-104, 106
Vosseller, Miss 28
Waldin, Jean (see Norman)
Waldorf Conference: Cultural and Scientific Conference for World Peace 81
Walls, J. W. 144
Walter, Francis E. 89-92, 94-96
Warsaw Ghetto 82
Washington, John 17, 92
Washington, Martha (formerly Custis, née Dandridge)
Webster, Margaret 75
Wells, H. G. 62
Wesley AME Zion Church 144
Weston, Lydia (see Cardozo)
Whitfield, Narcissa (see Robeson)
Williams, Sarah (see Congleton)
Williamston Township, Martin County, NC 135
Witherspoon Street Presbyterian Church, Princeton, New Jersey 13, 19, 25, 138
Witherspoon Street Public School, Princeton, New Jersey 30
Woodrow Wilson, Thomas 25
Wright, Richard 74
Wynn, Sally Rebecca (see Roberson)
YMCA (Young Men's Christian Association) 42-44
YWCA (Young Women's Christian Association) 42, 44

Zedong, Mao 86

About the Author

Andrew Norman was born in Newbury, Berkshire, UK in 1943. Having been educated at Thornhill High School, Gwelo, Southern Rhodesia (now Zimbabwe), Midsomer Norton Grammar School, and St Edmund Hall, Oxford, he qualified in medicine at the Radcliffe Infirmary. He has two children Bridget and Thomas, by his first wife.

From 1972-83, Andrew worked as a general practitioner in Poole, Dorset, before a spinal injury cut short his medical career. He is now an established writer whose published works include biographies of Charles Darwin, Winston Churchill, Thomas Hardy, T. E. Lawrence, Adolf Hitler, Agatha Christie, Enid Blyton, Beatrix Potter, Marilyn Monroe, and Sir Arthur Conan Doyle. Andrew married his second wife Rachel, in 2005.

Author's website: https://www.andrew-norman.co.uk

Lightning Source UK Ltd.
Milton Keynes UK
UKHW020631050422
401089UK00006B/145